RHYMES & REASONS

Literature and Language Play
for Phonological Awareness

Michael F. Opitz

HEINEMANN
Portsmouth, NH

Heinemann
A division of Reed Elsevier Inc.
361 Hanover Street
Portsmouth, NH 03801-3912
www.heinemann.com

Offices and agents throughout the world

CIP data is on file with the Library of Congress.
ISBN: 0-325-00246-0

Editor: Lois Bridges
Production: Merrill Peterson/Matrix Productions and Vicki Kasabian
Cover design: Monty Lewis
Manufacturing: Deanna Richardson

Printed in the United States of America on acid-free paper
04 03 02 01 00 DA   3 4 5

For children—my best teachers

Contents

Acknowledgments

This acknowledgments page is perhaps the most difficult for me to write. So many individuals work to turn a manuscript into a book, and I am always overwhelmed by the amount of support I receive when I write. I always fear that the words I choose to acknowledge individuals will seem inadequate. With this fear in mind, I offer my thanks to each of you.

Thanks, Sheryl, my wife, for keeping me moving by taking care of so many details. You made the completion of this book possible.

Thanks, Lois Bridges, my editor, for providing support in every conceivable way. From the proposal stage to selecting the perfect title for the finished manuscript, your specific and immediate responses to my drafts and ideas brought clarity and greater understanding. You are the kind of writing teacher I yearn to be.

Thanks, colleague Sandra Wilde, Portland State University, and teachers from Sweetwater School District #1: Amy Cheese, Mary Kay Cook, Joni Furman, Janet Geeting, Terri Hueckstaedt, Tina Johnson, Doris Lehman, Jan McIntosh, Josephine Profaizer, and Ilene Rutter for providing insightful comments on earlier drafts. And thanks, Barb Brewer for listening and responding to different ideas.

Thanks, publishers, for providing me with books to review and cite in this volume: Aladdin; Barefoot; Boyds Mills; Candlewick Press; Charlesbridge; Clarion; Crown; DK; Dutton; Farrar, Straus, & Giroux; Greenwillow; Grosset & Dunlap; Harcourt Brace; HarperCollins; Holiday House; Houghton Mifflin; Hyperion; Knopf; Lee & Low; Little, Brown; Lodestar; Lothrop; Morrow; Mulberry; North-South; Orchard; Pinata; Price/Stern/ Sloan; Penguin/Putnam; Scholastic; Simon & Schuster; Stoddart; Tambourine; Ticknor & Fields; Tricycle; and Viking.

Thanks, Jan McDearmon, for doing such an excellent job of copy-editing my manuscript. I learned from your work.

And thanks, Heinemann staff, for working on my behalf. I am greatly indebted to each of you—Michael Gibbons, Leigh Peake, Maura Sullivan, Vicki Kasabian, Louise Richardson, and Dan Breslin—for your unique contributions.

Introduction

Saturday morning brings me to yet another teacher audience interested in learning about phonological awareness. I ready myself and the group by reading a story that I will return to later in the day to emphasize how the text's language features help nurture phonological awareness in children in an enjoyable and meaningful way. Participants focused, I move to two of the most important activities of the day: inviting participants to think about and to share what they want to learn about phonological awareness.

"So," I say. "Instead of staying home doing the many tasks that call your name on this beautiful Saturday, you have chosen to devote the day to phonological awareness. What is it that you would like to know? What would you like to take away with you by the end of our time together? Please reflect on these two questions and write your responses. We'll then do some sharing and make a group list. This list will form the framework for today's session."

Pencils poised, they begin to write as I circulate, breaking a rule I was taught as a child—never read over the shoulders of a writer. I find it necessary, though, as it helps me to get a feel for my audience and to anticipate what they might ask. I also find it comforting because, invariably, questions I have seen and addressed before begin to show themselves; they mirror the objectives I have set for the day. We're in sync!

Feelings of relief, excitement, and enthusiasm energize me as I ask them to share some of their questions. I open up the sharing by stating the ground rules: "Now that all of you have had time to write down a few questions, let's get some of these up here on this chart. When you feel that your question logically follows the question being asked, please chime in." One by one, common questions emerge. Virginia takes the lead.

"I need some definitions," she says, and continues by clarifying what she means. "I sometimes hear people talking about phonological aware-ness and others talking about phonemic awareness. Are they the same?"

"I would add phonics to that," Ed adds. "I'm wondering if phonemic awareness is the same thing as phonics. Phonics has such negative conno-tations, I figure people have come up with the term 'phonemic awareness' as a more pleasant way of saying phonics. Is there a difference?"

"I have been teaching for over twenty years and seldom has one single topic been talked about as much as this one. I want to know why some are all hyped up about phonological awareness. I guess I need to know if I should be hyped up, too," Bill responds.

Sheryl joins the sharing: "I'll tell you why they're hyped, Bill, and why you should be, too. If what I've heard is true, phonological awareness is im-portant for children to become good readers. If children don't have it, they won't be able to read. I want to find out if this is true and, if so, how I can best teach it."

"My question relates to Sheryl's," Cathy says. "I've been teaching kin-dergarten and first grade for many years, and I have always believed in us-ing nursery rhymes, poetry, songs, and children's literature to help children learn more about how words work. It seems to work for me. Have I been doing right by my students? They appear to be doing okay, but maybe I'm missing something."

Other questions surface, variations of those listed above. I tell them that all of their questions and then some will be answered by the end of the day and that they will leave with an understanding of both phonologi-cal awareness and how to best develop it. This understanding will be ac-complished through the many activities they will experience, including a close look at recently published children's literature. And so another staff development session about phonological awareness—what it is and isn't and the best practices for fostering it—unfolds.

As the above scenario shows, there are many questions about phono-logical awareness and how best to develop it. In fact, this book evolved from questions such as these, coupled with my own teaching experiences and much reading on this topic. The book addresses common questions to en-able teachers to make informed decisions about the appropriateness of in-tegrating phonological awareness activities into their language arts pro-grams. But make no mistake! The primary purpose of this book is to call attention to recently published children's literature that can be used to foster children's understandings of phonological awareness in enjoyable and meaningful contexts. My goal is to provide a resource for busy teachers to access quality literature and to provide kid-tested, practical suggestions that will engage children and further finesse their phonological awareness. Children's literature is a delightful catalyst to nurture phonological awareness. As children play with rhymes and reasons, they will come to understand how knowledge of their language contributes to successful and enjoyable reading experiences.

The book is divided into eight chapters. The first chapter provides the grounding for the books and teaching suggestions that appear in Chapters 2–7—the major part of the book. In Chapter 1, I address common questions about phonological awareness such as those mentioned in the scenario above. I then address why there is so much concern about phonological awareness and why many people are confused by it. The chapter closes with best practices for fostering phonological awareness and suggestions for how to use this book.

Chapters 2–7 provide descriptions of children's literature that can be used to foster phonological awareness. Complete bibliographic information, including the ISBN number, is included with each annotation. I used specific criteria to select the books for each chapter, many of which were first listed by Yopp (1995). All of the books

- feature some sort of language play so that children's attention can focus on both the author's intended meaning and the language that the author uses to communicate the ideas (e.g., rhyme and alliteration). In this way, children can experience the delight and sensation of having sounds roll off their tongues, out of their mouths, and into their ears.
- lend themselves to further language exploration activities (signaled by a horn icon) and other book extension ideas (signaled by an open-book icon). These are sprinkled throughout Chapters 3–7. All of the activities are a natural outgrowth of the words used in the text and the ideas they convey. In this way, the authenticity of the literature selection is honored while at the same time the text serves as a springboard for instruction related to specific language features. The activities are intended to be used only after children have experienced any given book for sheer enjoyment.
- provide content that is appropriate for young children. Both the vocabulary and the ideas presented are suitable for children in the primary grades.
- are intended as read-alouds (although some children may be able to read them themselves!). In this way, all children can focus on the author's intended meaning and oral-language features, both of which lay the groundwork for successful independent reading experiences.

- are authentic texts. That is, the books are written to communicate ideas to the intended audience rather than to use specific words a given number of times.
- can be purchased in a bookstore or can be found in local libraries. In other words, they are children's trade books (i.e., books written to be read to, by, or with children).

Chapter 8 provides thirty phonological-awareness activities. Many of these activities can be used as you and your students wait for a guest speaker, get ready to leave for home, or ride the bus to a field trip. With some modification, many of the activities can also be used with several of the books shown in Chapters 2–7.

As you read through the various activities, please keep in mind that all suggestions are just that — suggestions. Use those that will work best for you and your students, and skip those that won't. You will also discover that each book lends itself to many different uses. You may decide, for instance, that you want to use an activity shown in Chapter 8 with one of the books rather than the ideas that are listed for the books in Chapters 2–7. I encourage you to do so and also encourage you to use any or all of the ideas listed in this book to spark your own ideas. In any case, use the books and the teaching suggestions to convey this most important message to our youth: learning about the sounds of our language is an enjoyable, rewarding activity that helps us to be independent lifelong readers.

Happy reading!

1

Getting Grounded

Firsthand teaching experiences, working with novice and veteran teachers, and reading related research literature (e.g., Bond and Dykstra 1967; Wharton-McDonald, Pressley, and Hampston 1998; Duffy and Hoffman 1999; Neuman 1999; Snow, Burns, and Griffin 1998) have led me to one conclusion: *knowledgeable teachers make a difference; there is no substitute.* The intent of this chapter, then, is to add to your knowledge base by sorting out the confusion surrounding phonological awareness. Doing so will better enable you to make informed decisions about when and whether to integrate phonological awareness activities into your language arts program. Let's begin with some definitions.

Defining Phonological Awareness, Phonemic Awareness, and Phonics

There *is* a difference between phonological awareness and phonemic awareness; they are not synonyms. And there *is* a difference between phonemic awareness and phonics; phonemic awareness is not a politically correct term for phonics. Let me explain.

Phonological awareness refers to awareness of many aspects of spoken language. These include the awareness of the following basic sound units:

- words within sentences
- syllables within words
- phonemes within syllables and words

Those who investigate and write about phonological awareness agree that phonological awareness is developmental—it develops in stages, the

5

first and easiest being the awareness that our language is composed of words. Language learners then progress to the stage in which they become aware that words are made up of word parts (i.e., syllables). The last and most difficult stage is one in which language learners become aware that syllables are made up of individual sounds (i.e., phonemes) (Liberman, Shankweiler, Fischer, and Carter 1974; Rozin and Gleitman 1977; Leong and Haines 1978; Morais 1991; Cunningham 2000). Figure 1–1 shows the different stages and sample tasks associated with each.

Phonemic awareness refers to the awareness that words are made up of individual sounds. It is one aspect of the larger category of phonological awareness and, as stated above and shown below, is the last stage through which children progress in terms of understanding their spoken language. Those investigating this topic agree that many tasks are associated with phonemic awareness and that some are more difficult than others (e.g.,

Phonological Awareness Task	*Sample Exercise*
Recognizing that words represent a sound unit — word awareness.	Children are provided with some sort of counters, such as peanuts and a small container. After reading a story to students, the teacher selects a sentence and says it aloud. The sentence is then slowly repeated and the students are asked to drop a peanut into their bag every time they hear a word.
Detecting that words are made up of different parts — syllables.	After reading through a story, the teacher selects some words that have single and multiple syllables and invites students to clap out the parts as individual words are read aloud.
Recognizing that words are made up of individual sounds — phonemes.	The teacher states a given word from a story and asks students how many sounds they hear in the word.

FIGURE 1–1. *Phonological Awareness Tasks and Sample Exercises*

Adams 1990; Yopp 1988; Griffith and Olson 1992). Identifying and producing rhyme and alliteration (i.e., words that begin alike) are the least difficult tasks, whereas those that require the child to segment the phonemes in a given word and manipulate phonemes to create new words appear to be more difficult. Figure 1–2 lists these tasks along with sample activities

Phonemic Awareness Task	*Sample Exercise*
Rhyme recognition: hearing and recognizing rhymes.	"Listen to this poem and tell me the rhyming words you hear."
Phoneme matching: identifying words that have a given sound (i.e., alliteration) or generating a word that has a given sound at the beginning, middle, or end.	*Alliteration:* "Listen to this sentence and tell me how all the words begin." *Generating words:* "Let's name some words that begin with /s/."*
Phoneme blending: putting sounds together to form a word.	"I'm thinking of a word that names an animal. It is a /k/ at. What's the word?" (cat) OR "It is a /k/ /a/ /t/."
Phoneme segmentation: isolating sounds at the beginning of a word or in an entire word. Sometimes the task requires hearing and counting; other times it requires producing the actual sounds.	*Hearing and Counting:* "Tell me how many sounds you hear in the word *dog.*" (3) *Producing sounds:* "Tell me the sounds you hear in the word *man.*" /m/, /a/, /n/
Phoneme manipulation: substituting, adding, or deleting sounds to create new words.	*Substituting:* "What word do we have if we change the /k/ in cat to /m/?" (mat) *Adding:* "Add /k/ to row. What's the name of our bird?" (crow) *Deleting:* "Take away the first sound in *cat.* What's your new word?" (at)
*a letter bounded by slashes denotes the sound associated with the letter	

FIGURE 1–2. *Phonemic Awareness Tasks and Sample Exercises*

associated with each. In essence, children are fully phonemically aware when they can manipulate and play with the sounds used to make words.

One important point to keep in mind is that phonemic awareness involves speech sounds rather than the letters that represent them. Said another way, a person can be phonemically aware yet unable to identify a single letter of the alphabet!

Another important point to consider is that phonemes are often distorted when we isolate them. This is one reason that sound-isolation activities are somewhat more difficult than identifying words within sentences and syllables within a word.

Phonics refers to the connection between sound and letter. When readers can connect a sound with the symbol that represents it, they are using phonics. Thus, a youngster who can "sound out" a word such as *dog* is using phonics.

Phonics Task	Sample Exercise
Decoding a word with a given number of sounds.	"Take a look at this word. Use what you know about letters and sounds to sound it out."

As these definitions show, each of these terms means something different. Understanding the terms as they are defined, then, seems a logical starting point for effective teaching.

Explaining the Hype

Yes, there is hype surrounding phonological awareness in general and phonemic awareness in particular. Here's why: If children are exposed to a rich language environment in which they enjoy read-alouds, songs, nursery rhymes, poems, and other forms of language play, most acquire some aspects of phonological awareness with relative ease at a very young age. In fact, some acquire all levels of phonological awareness before they even start school (Snow et al. 1998). However, some do not. The area of phonological awareness that these children appear to lack is phonemic awareness.

Lacking phonemic awareness concerns some researchers, educators, and those in other arenas because of the results of some studies conducted related to phonemic awareness and reading. For example, a study conducted by Juel (1988) showed that children who were lacking phonemic awareness in first grade were more likely to have reading difficulties in fourth grade. (See Adams [1990] for a review of other related studies). Findings such as these have led many to conclude that phonemic awareness is a necessary ingredient for successful reading. In fact, some believe that phonemic awareness is the greatest predictor of reading success, and they have research studies to support their beliefs. That is, those children who have phonemic awareness are more likely to succeed in reading than those who do not.

That findings and conclusions such as these have catapulted phonemic awareness into the media spotlight is no surprise. After all, we all want our children to succeed in reading and we are always on the lookout for the best ways to help them achieve this goal. Phonemic awareness appears to be important for successful reading.

Overcoming Confusion

If phonemic awareness is important, why don't we get on with helping children who need it "get it"? Why, instead, do I encounter individuals who are confused by its meaning and its relationship to reading? Much reflection on this question has led me to several sound reasons. Perhaps one of the best ways to overcome the confusion is to examine each one. Here, then, are reasons for the confusion. Perhaps yours mirror mine or you have additional reasons to add to my list.

Reasons for the confusion surrounding phonological awareness

1. *Definitions of reading vary.* Some individuals define reading as the ability to decode and identify words; most, however, define it as comprehension. In fact, most agree that there is no reading unless the reader takes away an understanding of the author's intended meaning. Nonetheless, the research findings that link phonemic awareness to reading success adopt a definition of reading that emphasizes segmenting sounds so that students will be able to decode words. For example, the International Reading Association Board of Directors (1998) notes that recent studies have shown "that the acquisition of phonemic awareness is highly predictive of success in learning to read—*in particular in predicting success in learning to decode*" (emphasis added). But what about the children who score well on phonological measures yet not so well on measures of reading comprehension?

Are they, too, good readers? The problem stems from the definition of reading that exists within the body of phonological research as a whole. Reading is much more than a precise process of word identification. Let me be clear. I am not suggesting that we throw away our advances in understanding phonological awareness and how it might relate to reading acquisition. Instead, I am suggesting that we can better understand the findings by explicitly defining what we mean when we use the terms *reading* and *reader*. In this way, teachers can more effectively help all children reach their full potential as strategic, competent readers. We must remember that reading is a complex behavior.

2. *Terms associated with phonological awareness are misused.* In some publications, instructional materials, and presentations I have read or attended, the terms *phonological awareness*, *phonemic awareness*, and *phonics* are often used as synonyms. Clearly, they are not. As shown above, each has its own distinct definition. Like Morais (1991), I believe that misuse of the terms has created much unnecessary ambiguity, which has hampered the study of how literacy acquisition and phonemic awareness might be related.

3. *Children defy our knowledge.* While there is agreement among educators that some level of phonemic awareness is important for reading success, there are children who learn to read very well without it. Take deaf children, for example. Most learn to read quite well, yet they cannot hear sounds (Luckner 1999). Likewise, some children comprehend everything they read and therefore are excellent readers yet do not fare so well on phonemic awareness tasks and tests. If phonemic awareness fosters reading success, how can these children succeed? Clearly, children such as these remind us that the search to account for reading success is not over.

4. *Phonemic awareness activities sometimes lead those who purchase them astray.* The marketplace is currently being flooded with materials that teachers can purchase and use to teach phonemic awareness explicitly. Often these materials include phonics activities rather than phonemic awareness activities. Consider, for example, this activity that is said to teach youngsters how to segment sounds in words. It states, "Practice decoding some of the words that children have been able to segment" (Ericson and Juliebo 1998, 57). Clearly, this is a phonics activity because decoding requires matching sounds to the letters that represent them.

5. *Some published materials promote the mistaken belief that there is a set sequence of activities through which children must progress in order to become phonemically aware*. True, there are different types of tasks associated with phonemic awareness, but there is no proven sequence for completion of these tasks. And we have yet to discover how much phonemic awareness is necessary for successful reading (Coles 2000). The only conclusion that can be drawn from the research literature is something that experienced teachers have known for quite some time: *children appear to hear rhyming words and words that begin the same first*. They then show the ability to hear, blend, and isolate individual sounds (i.e., phonemes) in words (Eldridge 1995). Once again, though, as experienced teachers know, children defy our categories. Some are unable to perform a "prerequisite" for a more advanced task yet have no difficulty completing the advanced task!

Likewise, there is no research that supports the idea of having children show mastery of a given phonemic awareness task by completing a set number of workbook exercises before they can move on to the next task. Furthermore, there is no research that supports the notion that children must first be able to hear sounds in nature as a prerequisite to hearing sounds in syllables and words.

Finally, much of the research that is often used to create phonological awareness intervention programs reflects actual classroom practice the least. A thorough review of thirty-nine studies focused on phonological intervention, for example, led Troia (1999) to conclude that "we do not have adequate evidence that phonological awareness treatment programs are ecologically valid and effective in classroom environments. It is possible that such programs may be too impractical or too complex for implementation in the classroom and that the positive effects observed by researchers would be compromised in classroom practice" (49).

6. *There are conflicting views about how and when phonemic awareness develops*. At the present time, few dispute the notion that phonemic awareness is related to reading success. However, this is about the only point of agreement. Different theorists have designed and conducted studies to discover just how and when children learn phonemic awareness. Their studies have led them to different explanations with accompanying research findings to support their views. Figure 1–3 lists these views, the belief statement of those who hold each view, and research that is used to support the view. Is it any wonder that we are so confused?

11

Although these different views exist, the reciprocal view is supported by the majority of researchers (Yopp 1992; Weaver 1998). In fact, the findings of Linda Ayers' award-winning study (1993) led her to conclude: "Students whose phonological awareness is less than completely developed are nevertheless capable of making progress in reading" (150). Snow et al. (1998) echo this conclusion:

> In sum, despite the theoretical importance of phonological awareness for learning to read, its predictive power is somewhat muted, because, at about the time of the onset of school, so many children who will go on to become normally achieving readers have not yet attained much, if any, appreciation of the phonological structure of oral language. (112)

View	Belief Statement	Supporting Research
Prerequisite	Progress in reading is not possible unless learners know that words have sounds and that these sounds are attached to letters.	Bradley and Bryant 1985; Fox and Routh 1976; Golinkoff 1978; Juel, Griffith, and Gough 1986
Consequence	Phonemic awareness is acquired as a result of learning to read.	Ehri 1979; Ehri and Wilce 1980; Morais, Carey, Alegria, and Bertelson 1979
Facilitative	Phonemic awareness is a necessary skill yet not sufficient in learning how to read.	Goldstein 1976; Tunmer and Nesdale 1985; Ehri 1979
Reciprocal	Phonemic awareness helps children learn to read, and learning to read helps children become phonemically aware.	Liberman, Shankweiler, Fischer, and Carter 1974; Perfetti, Beck, Bell, and Hughes 1987; Ayers 1993

Figure 1–3. *Views of Phonemic Awareness*

Fostering Phonological Awareness: Best Practices

For the majority of children, phonological awareness is more caught than taught. Children who "catch it" are exposed to a rich language environment (e.g., home, preschool) in which they enjoy read-alouds, songs, nursery rhymes, poems, and other forms of language play long before formal schooling begins. However, even for these children, phonological awareness is anything but all-or-nothing. They continue to refine this awareness through reading and writing experiences provided in the primary grades (Snow et al. 1998). Likewise, they take great pleasure in language play activities because they have already grasped an understanding of how their language works. They understand that playing with their language is an enjoyable experience that leads to greater understanding of it. But what about the children who lack these experiences or those who have had these experiences yet still lack phonological awareness? What are we to do to foster their phonological awareness?

A close look at children who "catch" phonological awareness provides a hint as to how we can best nurture phonological awareness in those who don't. That is, we need to provide them with an oral language–rich environment—one that includes read-alouds, songs, nursery rhymes, poems, and other forms of language play. And, fortunately for these children, many of these activities already exist in classrooms (Griffith and Olson 1992). But this is not enough. These children also need what *all* children need to make sense of how language works—a print-rich environment that affords them with many opportunities to participate in authentic reading and writing experiences. Fortunately, there are some best practices that can be drawn from the research base to ensure that all children receive appropriate instruction. These are as follows:

1. *Embed phonological awareness into everyday reading and writing experiences.* The necessity of embedding phonological awareness into language arts programs that include many different types of literacy experiences is underscored many times (e.g., Griffith and Olson 1992; Ayers 1993; Neuman 1999; Cunningham 1990; Richgels et al. 1996). Figure 1–4 lists typical reading and writing experiences, a sample activity for each, and how the experience promotes phonological awareness.

2. *Provide time for children to write and allow for invented spelling.* While phonological awareness is focused on sounds of language rather than its

13

Typical Reading/ Writing Experiences	Sample Activity	Phonological Awareness
Read-aloud	Reading books that emphasize language features such as rhyme and alliteration.	Words are made up of sound elements that sometimes sound alike.
Shared reading	Reading a big book and asking children to clap every time they hear a word.	Words are separate units in the speech stream. They can be used to create stories and sentences.
Guided reading	Providing children with a text to read and directing them to point to each word as they read.	Stories are made up of words. Spaces show where the word starts and ends.
Independent reading	Providing time for children to read their own books.	Stories are a written form of language. There are units of sound in the speech stream—including words, syllables, and sounds—that are used to write these stories.
		(continued)

Figure 1–4. *Reading and Writing Experiences That Foster Phonological Awareness*

printed form, a wealth of research points to the value of writing to further develop phonological awareness (Snow et al. 1998; Clay 1998; Cunningham 1990; Tangel and Blachman, 1992; Ehri and Wilce 1987; Clarke 1988; Wilde 1997). Griffith (1991) provides one explanation for how this happens: "While writing, young children directly confront the problem of representing spoken language with written language and must out of necessity develop the ability to segment phonemes" (231). In fact, Snowball and

Typical Reading/ Writing Experiences	Sample Activity	Phonological Awareness
Modeled writing	Inviting children to watch as words are written on a chart or the board, saying each slowly to stretch them out— either by syllable or by sound.	Several word parts/ sounds can be used to create a word. These need to be put in a specific sequence.
Interactive writing	Encouraging children to participate in creating a message by stating their ideas.	Speech can be written. It is written in chunks.
Independent writing	Providing time for children to write.	Sounds are used to create words to communicate an idea to others.

FIGURE 1–4, *continued*

Bolton (1999) suggest that looking at children's writing is one of the best ways to determine levels of phonological awareness. Those writings that show spaces between words and words constructed using representative symbols for sounds indicate that the writer has most likely developed a sense of all levels of phonological awareness described earlier (see pages 5–8). On the other hand, if strings of letters and other symbols make up the writing, the writer needs to become more phonologically aware. Wilde (1999) notes that children who are phonetic-invented spellers are phonemically aware and thus need no further explicit instruction.

3. *Read aloud children's literature that focuses on specific language features.* Reading aloud children's literature that focuses on specific language elements is one of the best ways to foster phonological awareness (Neuman 1999; Murray et al. 1996; Hoffman 1997; Griffith and Olson 1992; Yopp 1992; Ayers 1993; Griffith 1991). Texts such as these draw learners' attention to given language features such as rhyme, alliteration, phoneme

substitution, and phoneme segmentation. Griffith and Olson (1992) comment: "In addition to pure enjoyment, sound-play books heighten a child's sensitivity to the phonological structure of language. Some children may be able to discover and attend to sounds in language as a result of the linguistic stimulation provided by these kinds of books. Indeed, children who have enjoyed extensive storybook exchanges may develop phonemic awareness without direct instruction" (521). Most recently, this comment is supported by Neuman's (1999) findings.

4. *Use fun, engaging oral language activities.* Some children may need more explicit instruction to develop all levels of phonological awareness. However, this need not be an isolated chore or bore. The activities can and should be an extension of a literacy experience so that children can see how the activity connects to reading and writing (Bear, Invernizzi, Templeton, and Johnston 2000; Cunningham 1990; Eldredge 1995; Ayers 1993; Yopp 1995; Snow et al. 1998). Yopp states, "Phonemic awareness should not be addressed as an abstract isolated skill to be acquired through drill type activities. It can be a natural, functional part of literacy experiences throughout the day" (27). In fact, the results of some studies have shown that children who engage in meaningful, connected activities actually perform as well as or (most often) better on phonological awareness tasks than children who complete isolated activities (Ayers 1993; Neuman 1999; Cunningham 1990).

5. *Determine what students need.* Good teaching of phonological awareness is no different from any other effective teaching: it is based on what children know and need to know. Rather than haphazardly choosing any activity, then, effective teachers take their cues from their students to best help them become competent readers.

6. *Involve families.* The findings of many studies related to parental involvement and its impact on several aspects of literacy point to the need to invite parental participation (see Snow et al. [1998, 138–47] for a review of these studies; Whitehurst et al. 1988). Nonetheless, my teaching experiences have helped me see that, while they want to help, parents are not quite sure how or what to do—they need some "know-how." Rather than overwhelm parents by providing them with an entire list of books and ideas, choose a title shown in this book and one activity and provide a brief explanation for how to complete the activity. Gradually, over time, you will teach them how to complete numerous appropriate activities designed to

Dear Parents,

Becoming aware of how our spoken language works and how this relates to reading is one aspect of developing as an accomplished reader. One of the best ways for children to develop this understanding is to hear stories—especially those that encourage language play through the use of rhyme and alliteration. The enclosed book makes much use of rhyme. Here are some suggestions for using it:

1. Read the book to your child for enjoyment.

2. Read the book again and pause when you come to a word that rhymes with one used in the preceding sentence. Ask your child to state a word that would make sense and that rhymes with one given in the line above. If your child cannot tell you, go ahead and tell him or her. Remember, the ability to hear rhyming words is more caught than taught!

Thank you for your willingness to help your child become a better reader by reading this book and completing this activity.

Sincerely,
Your Child's Teacher

FIGURE 1–5. *Sample Letter to Parents*

heighten phonological awareness. The letter shown in Figure 1–5 is a sample that can be used to do just that. Once you have shown them how to complete the various activities, you might want to send home a form such as the one in Figure 1–6. Keep in mind that this is only a sample and that you will most likely need to modify it to fit your needs. For example, you may want to include other types of phonological tasks on the grid. In this way, parents can note the date, title, and activities that were completed. Talk about meaningful homework—here it is!

Using This Book

All of the books I include in this volume can be used for a variety of purposes. At no time should you feel that you must use the books in every section, some before others; the order in which they are presented is simply an organizational scheme. In fact, a close reading will show that the books in each section are alphabetized by title. Likewise, I sincerely hope that all will use this book to best advance students' knowledge. If, however, you

Child's name _____

Date	Title of Book	States words that rhyme; generates another rhyming word	Identifies alliteration; states another word that begins the same	Takes off the beginning sound and adds another to create a new word	Other observations

Figure 1–6. *Parents' Observation Record*

want to use the books to help children develop a given aspect of phono-logical awareness that appears lacking, I suggest the procedures listed be-low when using this book. Also, keep in mind that phonological awareness activities need to be integrated into the larger language arts curriculum.

1. *Identify the specific phonological awareness task that needs to be addressed* (see pages 6 – 7 for a listing of these tasks). Only you will be able to best de-termine what your students need based on your observations of them as they interact with print in various literacy experiences.

2. *Select a book from Chapters 2–7 that will help address this need.* There are many titles from which to choose, and choose you must! You will most likely use some of the books but certainly not all of them — nor should you feel obligated to do so. In other words, I have made every attempt to include a variety of books within each category to provide choice rather than sug-gest a mandate that all be used.

3. *Engage the children with the book.* Here are some suggestions that are sure to invite success (based on Yopp [1995]):

- Remember that enjoyment is the first step. Encourage all children to par-ticipate by gathering them together, showing the book to them, and inviting their predictions based on their observations of the book cover.
- Read the book to your students one or two — even three or four times if you want — before you focus on the language used in the story.
- Call children's attention to the language used in the story. You may want to use a specific phonological awareness activity mentioned for the book you selected (signaled by the musical horn icon) or an activity from Chapter 8 to call attention to the language feature. You may instead want to call attention to the language feature more informally by simply com-menting on what the author is doing. For example, for a book in which much rhyming is used, you might comment, "*Bed, red.* Hey! Those words rhyme! This author uses a lot of rhyming words in this book."
- Complete additional activities to extend the book. You may want to use the book to extend the students' learning in some way. If so, you may find the book extenders (signaled by the open-book icon) helpful. Take *A Pinky Is a Baby Mouse*, for example. You may want to have students com-plete the book extender as explained on page 27 to provide them with an opportunity to generate and state clues about a given animal to further their facility with spoken language while at the same time furthering their knowledge of animals.

4. *Display the book during independent reading time.* Some children will want to look at the book during their independent reading time. Some will pretend to read the book, making up the story as best as they can recall. Others will actually read the story as it is printed. Providing children with these experiences is an excellent way to help them connect spoken and written language. As Roberts (1992) noted, "Understanding the characteristics of *word* as defined by a literate society evolves from experience with print" (136).

2

Rhyming Texts

Is it any wonder that most children develop a sense of rhyme with relative ease? After all, they are surrounded by rhyme in their everyday lives through the songs they are sung by their parents or those they hear while viewing television and movies. And think about the many nursery rhymes and rhythmic texts that are read aloud to them! Not surprisingly, then, children develop an ear for rhyme if they are provided with opportunities to hear it. And for those children who haven't had such opportunities, immerse them in the delightful books filled with rhyme. Those most recently published are included in this section. You can provide more explicit attention to rhyme and other aspects of spoken language by using the activities that follow given titles.

———————————◆———————————

A Was Once an Apple Pie
Edward Lear, Author
Julie Lacome, Illustrator
Cambridge, MA: Candlewick. 1997. 0-7636-0103-9.

Here is a series of nonsense verses that help children experience the fun of language by inviting them to play with sound and rhythm. Each letter of the alphabet is represented by a nonsense verse, primarily created by substituting various initial sounds in the words used to create the rhyme.

Focus on Phonological Awareness (phoneme substitution): A sample rhyme from this book shows that the rhyme is created by changing the initial sound (i.e., phoneme substitution):

21

A was once an apple pie,
  Pidy
  Widy
  Tidy
  Pidy
Nice insidy Apple pie.

A logical follow-up, then, is to provide children with different letters of the alphabet and encourage them to create similar rhymes for their letter. This activity can be easily modified to a whole-group activity by placing all the letters in a bag, choosing a child to select one from the bag, and asking the class to create a rhyme for it.

The Absentminded Fellow
Samuel Marshak, Author
Translated from Russian by Richard Pevear
Marc Rosenthal, Illustrator
New York: Farrar, Straus & Giroux. 1999. 0-374-300135.

Originally published in Russia in 1928, this is the story of an absent-minded fellow whose mishaps cause all sorts of confusion. Children will take delight in learning about what happens to the absentminded fellow throughout the day from the very beginning when they see him putting his trousers on his head and his shirt on his legs. Add to this the confusion that results when he mixes up words and students are sure to see the importance of using the correct sounds in words to communicate important information.

 Focus on Phonological Awareness (phoneme manipulation): Many of the words in this book encourage play with sounds because of the substitutions that are made. For example, instead of saying, "Driver, take me to the train!" the absentminded fellow states, "Driver, stake me to the drain." For each of the mixed-up words, ask students which sounds need to be taken away or added so that the words in the sentence will make sense.

☐ *Book Extender:* After each episode presented in the book, at least one person says, "Oh, that absentminded fellow from Portobello Road!"

Thus, this is a perfect book for shared reading. Invite students to say the phrase after you read the episode.·

America: My Land, Your Land, Our Land
W. Nikola-Lisa, Author
Illustrated by fourteen American artists
New York: Lee and Low. 1997. 1-88000-037-7.

Through simple two-word rhyming verse and illustrations that depict various cultural groups, readers experience the many characteristics of the United States. Pictures of the illustrators are accompanied by explanations of their illustrations and a brief biography of each.

The Baseball Counting Book
Barbara McGrath, Author
Brian Shaw, Illustrator
Watertown, MA: Charlesbridge. 1999. 0-88106-333-9.

Through simple rhyming verse, children will learn some baseball fundamentals as a result of listening to this book. Beginning with the essential materials needed to play the game and ending with the celebrations that happen after the game, McGrath encourages children to understand and play the game that is loved by many.

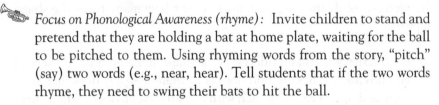 *Focus on Phonological Awareness (rhyme):* Invite children to stand and pretend that they are holding a bat at home plate, waiting for the ball to be pitched to them. Using rhyming words from the story, "pitch" (say) two words (e.g., near, hear). Tell students that if the two words rhyme, they need to swing their bats to hit the ball.

📖 *Book Extender:* This book is a natural for encouraging children to tell about their experiences with baseball and for inviting those who collect cards to share them with others. For those children who have never played the game, the book can be used as an introduction, followed by a trip outside to actually play the game.

Bear's Busy Family
Stella Blackstone, Author
Debbie Harter, Illustrator
New York: Barefoot. 1999. 1-902283-90-2.

Like most families, Bear's family completes many activities throughout a day. Using very simple rhyming text that also appeals to the senses, youngsters will discover these many activities. The book closes showing Bear's family tree.

Focus on Phonological Awareness (rhyme): During a second reading of this book, pause when you come to a word that rhymes with a word in the previous line and encourage students to chime in with the rhyming word.

Book Extender: This book lends itself to movements. Together with students, brainstorm gestures that can be used for each of the actions in the story. Once established, read the book again as they make the gestures that correspond to the actions.

Bear in a Square
Stella Blackstone, Author
Debbie Harter, Illustrator
New York: Barefoot. 1998. 1-901223-58-2.

With simple rhyming text, youngsters are encouraged to locate specific shapes that are used to create the lively illustrations in this text. The right-hand side of the page shows how many times a given shape appears in the picture, subtly inviting students to count how many times the shape appears.

Book Extender: Take children on a shape hunt around the school grounds asking them to find objects in their everyday lives that have various shapes. Providing each with a small tablet to record their "field notes" will go a long way toward helping them understand the importance of taking notes that can be used later. Once back in the classroom, show children a given shape and invite them to look through their field notes to locate any objects they observed that have the shape.

Bear on a Bike
Stella Blackstone, Author
Debbie Harter, Illustrator
New York: Barefoot. 1998. 1-901223-49-3.

With a little imagination, bears can travel to many different places, as this text shows. Using rhythmic, rhyming text, Blackstone invites children to join the journeys.

📖 *Book Extender:* This book is set up as a conversation and, as a result, lends itself well to choral reading. One group can take on the role of the child who asks the bear where he is going. The second group can take on the role of the bear by answering.

A Beasty Story
Bill Martin Jr. and Steven Kellogg, Authors
Steven Kellogg, Illustrator
San Diego: Harcourt. 1999. 0-15-201683-X.

A group of mice seek adventure by going into a dark wood, which leads them into a dark house. Once in the house, they discover many different objects, each a different color, that arouse their curiosity and lead them to the discovery of a monster that frightens them and causes them to run from the house. They run to another house where a young boy helps the mice see that the monster chasing them is nothing more than two balloons covered by a sheet.

🎺 *Focus on Phonological Awareness (rhyme):* The rhyming words in this text are *brown, down; strange, change; ahead, red; too, blue; guess, yes; jeepers, creepers; flies, eyes; trace, fireplace; track, stack; surprise, disguise.* Say each pair of words, asking students to clap if the two words rhyme.

Before I Go to Sleep
Thomas Hood, Author
Maryjane Begin, Illustrator
New York: Morrow. 1999 (reissue). 0-688-12424-0.

What do you do when it's too hot to go to sleep? The young boy in this text imagines that he is different kinds of animals as he waits for the night to cool down. Youngsters will take delight in the illustrations of the animals doing what the boy imagines he would do if he were the animal.

📖 *Book Extender:* Ask children what animal they would like to be if they could be one and to tell why. Next, provide them with a copy of their photograph and have them incorporate it into a drawing of themselves as the animal they would like to be doing the kinds of things they mention.

The Boy Who Longed for a Lift
Norma Farber, Author
Brian Selznick, Illustrator
New York: HarperCollins. 1997. 0-06-027108-6.

A young boy goes walking but soon grows tired of it and accepts rides from several different objects in nature. The river, for example, gives him a lift, and as he rides down it, a boat comes along just in time to give him a lift when the river gets too swift. Although he experiences many different rides, the one he enjoys most is the one his father provides — a loving lift!

📖 *Book Extender:* This is an excellent book for retelling events. Invite students to state the different ways that the boy received a lift. Once all of these are mentioned, ask students to state which lift was provided first, second, and so on. After each is mentioned, show them the text to verify their answers.

Butterfly House
Eve Bunting, Author
Greg Shed, Illustrator
New York: Scholastic. 1999. 0-590-84884-4.

A girl and her grandfather make a house for a larva. Together, they watch the larva turn into a beautiful butterfly, a "painted lady" as grandpa calls it, to be set free.

📖 *Book Extender:* Through the lyrical text, children learn much about the needs of larva if they are to turn into butterflies. Using the text as a guide, have children create their own larva containers. Provide them each with a larva and, just as the girl in the story does, have them feed it and observe any changes that occur. Children could also be provided with observation logs in which they can record the changes they see.

A Cake All for Me!
Karen Magnuson Beil, Author
Paul Meisel, Illustrator
New York: Holiday House. 1998. 0-8234-1368-3.

The ingredients for baking and sharing a cake are provided in this book as Piggy goes about creating a cake and sharing it with friends. Rhythmic text as well as themes and rhythms of other nursery rhymes are used to create a fun story to hear or read. Want to make your own polka-dot cake? You'll find the recipe and table of measurements in the back.

📖 *Book Extender:* Using the recipe in the back of the book, make the cake with your students.

A Pinky Is a Baby Mouse and Other Baby Animal Names
Pam Munoz Ryan, Author
Diane deGroat, Illustrator
New York: Hyperion. 1997. 0-7868-2190-6.

Rhyming verses are used to provide clues about the names of baby animals. Animals that live in the barnyard, forest, ocean, rainforest, Africa, and Australia are included in their natural habitats. In all, the text introduces more than one hundred creatures and their newborn names. A listing of animals and names given to the newborns is provided on the last two pages of the text.

 Focus on Phonological Awareness (syllables): Because the animal names used in the text are single- and multisyllabic, provide pictures of the various animals and have students classify them into those whose names have one part, two parts, and three parts:

One part: pig, goat, kid, squab, mouse, frog, crane, swan, owl, bat, pup, eel, seal, spike, calf, hawk, cub, foal, chick.
Two parts: piglet, pigeon, pinky, craneling, cygnet, kitten, owlet, glow-worm, firefly, elver, weaner, giraffe, zebra, spider, monkey, hatchling, joey, puggle, emu.
Three parts: fingerling, polliwog, jellyfish, ephyra, mackerel, spiderling, crocodile, neonate, kangaroo, anteater, platypus.

📖 *Book Extender:* Play match-up. Have students match names of baby animals with their adult name. Each name could be printed on an index card and placed in a pocket holder. Another way to play this game is to have the person holding the name of the newborn animal provide clues about himself. When finished, the child who thinks she has the adult name of the animal could stand up and join the "baby."

A Place to Bloom
Lorianne Siomades, Author and Illustrator
Honesdale, PA: Boyds Mills. 1997. 1-56397-656-0.

The message of this book is that the world exists for everyone. Some of the things that we dislike or discard may be another's treasure. In simple rhyme, youngsters are invited to explore the world around them more closely.

Focus on Phonological Awareness (rhyme): Play "I'm thinking" with students. Create riddles that can be answered by using rhyming words from this text. For example, "I'm thinking of a word that rhymes with *think*. It's what you do when you are thirsty." (*drink*)

Book Extender: Provide time for children to think about some of the things they dislike that could be treasures for others.

Baby Angels
Jane Cowen-Fletcher, Author and Illustrator
Cambridge, MA: Candlewick. 1996. 1-56402-666-3.

A young child seeks adventure, knowing that baby angels surround her to prevent her from harm. From the time she awakens and crawls out of bed to the many activities throughout the day, the baby angels perform miracles to keep the baby close to her loved ones.

Focus on Phonological Awareness (phoneme substitution): Using words from the book, say something like, "Take the /w/ off of *wake* and add /m/. What's the new word? (make)

Baby Born
Anastasia Suen, Author
Chih-Wei Chang, Illustrator
New York: Lee and Low. 1998. 1-880000-68-7.

Here is a book that celebrates the growth of a baby through the seasons. Using rhythmic text accompanied by watercolor illustrations, Suen takes the reader through the different seasons, showing how babies of different ethnic backgrounds grow. A lift of the flap on each page reveals a hidden surprise related to the verse.

📖 *Book Extender:* Invite students to make their own flip books to demonstrate their understanding of events that happen within each season. Each activity they put into their books could relate to their own lives.

This book can also be used to celebrate cultural diversity as many different ethnic groups are depicted in the illustrations. The text illustrates commonalities while at the same time honoring cultural differences.

Baby High, Baby Low
Stella Blackstone, Author
Denise Fraifeld and Fernando Azevedo, Illustrators
New York: Holiday House. 1998. 0-8234-1345-4.

Three babies complete many different activities, and through them, learners see how opposites work. *High/low*, *quick/slow*, and *happy/sad* are three of the ten opposites depicted in the text.

🎺 *Focus on Phonological Awareness/phonics (rhyme):* Using the rhyming words from the book, ask students to stand if the words you say rhyme and to stay seated if they don't. Example: "*Sad, bad,* Stand if they rhyme."

📖 *Book Extender:* Invite students to make their own books of opposites. Provide them with a blank book created by stapling a few sheets of white paper down the center. Provide magazines and crayons, and ask students to find pictures that show opposites, or encourage them to draw their own.

Baby Tamer
Mark Teague, Author and Illustrator
New York: Scholastic. 1997. 0-590-67712-8.

Like many children, the Eggmont children can cause havoc when their parents are away, intimidating the best of baby-sitters. And this is exactly what the children plan to do to the sitter their parents have hired for this evening. However, little do they know that they have met their match. The sitter their parents have hired is more than a sitter—she's a baby tamer! And this is exactly what she does. Most readers will agree with her when she states that she is "one cool cucumber."

Focus on Phonological Awareness (rhyme): On a second reading of this book, pause when you come to a word that rhymes with a word used at the end of the previous sentence or phrase. Invite children to state the word that rhymes.

📖 *Book Extender:* Ask children what they do when their parents leave them with a sitter. Or, better yet, have them tell what they might do if they were in charge of such unruly children.

Barn Cat
Carol Saul, Author
Mary Azarian, Illustrator
New York: Little, Brown. 1998. 0-316-76113-3.

In search of what she is looking for, Barn Cat seems oblivious to the many insects and animals around her. The woodcuts used to illustrate the various creatures provide readers with details of each. In addition to rhythmic text, this book is also a counting book.

📖 *Book Extender:* This book invites shared reading. Ask children to recite, in unison, the verse "Barn Cat at the red barn door, Barn Cat, what are you looking for?" The reader can then read the text to answer the question. Another way to extend the story is to provide students with a list of numbers 1–10 and ask them to recall the animals associated with each number in the text. Once they give their responses, verify by looking at the text.

Barnyard Song
Rhonda Gowler Greene, Author
Robert Bender, Illustrator
New York: Atheneum. 1997. 0-689-80758-9.

The animals on this farm get the barnyard flu, which causes their regular sounds to become distorted. One by one, the farmer cures the animals, enabling them to sing their sweetest barnyard songs ever.

 Focus on Phonological Awareness (rhyme): Play "odd one out" with students. Tell them that you will say three words from the text and that two of them rhyme and one does not. Tell them to listen to all three and state which one is the odd one out. For example, *"Day, hay, throats. Which one is odd one out?"* (*throats*)

📖 *Book Extender:* Provide pictures of the animals that appear in the story. Pass out the pictures to volunteers and have them line up according to the animal that appeared first, second, and so on, in the story.

Beach Play
Marsha Hayles, Author
Hideko Takahashi, Illustrator
New York: Holt. 1998. 0-8050-4271-7.

The beach offers many opportunities for play as this book well illustrates. Told in simple, bouncy, rhyming verse, this book will delight children with all the beach has to offer from early morning to late afternoon. The bright, vivid, acrylic illustrations enhance the text, making this a pleasing book to read.

 Focus on Phonological Awareness (rhyme): Tell students that you will state a set of words from the text and they are to tell you which one does not rhyme with the others—which one is the "odd word out."

Sample sets:
Set 1: smacking, packing, *sandy*, stacking
Set 2: *spreading*, lunching, munching
Set 3: *climbing*, dangling, tangling
Set 4: licking, *drippy*, sticking

Bear Day
Cynthia Rylant, Author
Jennifer Selby, Illustrator
San Diego: Harcourt. 1998. 0-15-201090-4.

From the moment he awakens to the end of the day, Bear accomplishes many things. Through rhyming text, youngsters learn about time sequence.

📖 *Book Extender:* Provide students with a sheet of paper divided into three parts and encourage them to draw or find a representative picture in a magazine that shows what they do in the morning, at midday, and in the evening.

The Bear Whose Bones Were Jezebel Jones
Bill Grossman, Author
Jonathan Allen, Illustrator
New York: Dial. 1997. 0-8037-1742-3.

One day a bear decides to take off his fur so that he can wash his bones. Along comes a child, Jezebel, who tries on the skin but can't take it off. In the end, her dog fetches a bunch of bones (could they be the bear's?) that unzips the skin to let Jezebel out and the bear back in.

Bearobics
Vic Parker, Author
Emily Bolam, Illustrator
New York: Viking. 1997. 0-670-87034-X.

A bear turns up the volume of his boom box to encourage the other jungle animals to join in some exercise—bearobics! Silly rhymes are used to introduce progressively larger numbers of animals into the jungle jive. Children will have trouble sitting still as they listen to this story. Invite them to snap their fingers and tap their toes as part of their own "bearobics"!

Focus on Phonological Awareness (syllables): Play "yes or no." Tell students that you will ask a question using some words from the book. If the last word in the question rhymes with a word mentioned earlier, the answer is yes; if not, the answer is no. For example: Does a bear breathe air? (yes) Does a bear rest? (no).

Book Extender: Having children dramatize this book by doing their own kidarobics is a natural extension of this book. Put on some music and have them get into their own jive!

The Beastly Feast
Bruce Goldstone, Author
Blair Lent, Illustrator
New York: Holt. 1998. 0-8050-3867-1.

Animals from everywhere come to a feast, each bringing a specific food to share and this is where the rhyming text fits in. That is, each animal brings a food that rhymes with its name. The antelope brings cantaloupe while the puffins bring muffins. After partaking in this feast, all clap and settle in for a nap!

Better Not Get Wet, Jesse Bear
Nancy White Carlstrom, Author
Bruce Degen, Illustrator
New York: Aladdin. 1997. 0-689-81055-5.

Jesse Bear decides to go wading. Along the way to the pool, he sees several animals getting wet. Finally, it's his turn to jump into the pool and get wet, both from the pool water and from the hose his father is using to squirt him.

Focus on Phonological Awareness (phoneme deletion): Some of the rhymes are created using sound deletion. Thus, this book lends itself well to sound deletion activities. Say, for example, "What sound did I take away from _____ to make _____?" Word pairs: *cup, up; spout, out; about, out; bear, air.*

The Biggest Snowball Ever!
John Rogan, Author and Illustrator
Cambridge, MA: Candlewick. 1998. 0-7636-0485-2.

Like most children, the children in this book enjoy playing in the snow and having snowball fights. And, as can often happen, one snowball leads to many other events. In this tale, the children themselves get caught inside a large out-of-control snowball and need to be freed so that they can be home in time to celebrate Christmas. The text incorporates many rhymes, making this a perfect book for developing children's ears for rhyming text.

Boo to a Goose
Mem Fox, Author
David Miller, Illustrator
New York: Dial. 1998. 0-8037-2274-5.

Here is the story of a young boy who will do many activities before he even thinks about saying boo to a goose. The many rhyming alternatives and the repetitive nature of the text are sure to encourage listeners and readers to create their own "silly goose" verses.

 Focus on Phonological Awareness (phoneme substitution): The rhyming verses in this text are primarily created using initial consonant substitution: *pig, wig; roo, Kalamazoo; mountain, fountain; snake, awake; snails, pails; whale, pale; street, feet; yellow, bellow; knees, bees; town, down; see, three.* Say each pair and ask children to state what is the same and what is different.

📖 *Book Extender:* Invite children to create their own silly goose verses using the same pattern as the one in the text. Then invite them to write and illustrate the verses. Compile these in a book entitled "Silly Goose Verses by the Silly Kids in Room _____."

Bowl Patrol
Marilyn Janovitz, Author and Illustrator
New York: North-South. 1996. 1-55858-636-9.

In this story, which uses fifteen rhyming pairs, a dog protects her water bowl from others who would like to use it. Finally, the dog learns that sharing causes a lot less stress and can be an enjoyable experience.

Camel Caravan
Bethany Roberts and Patricia Hubbell, Authors
Cheryl Munro Taylor, Illustrator
New York: Tambourine. 1996. 0-688-13939-6.

Five camels are sick and tired of having to carry such heavy loads across the desert. They set off in search of a new life via boxcar, bus, and bicycle, to name a few. In the end, they discover that the desert is where they long to be after all and return to "home sweet home."

 Focus on Phonological Awareness (phoneme blending): This is an excellent book to use to show how sounds at the beginning of words can change while the last part remains the same. Ask students to place different sounds in front of *-ump*. Then blend the entire word. For example, " /l/ /ump/. What's the word?"

Can I Help?
Marilyn Janovitz, Author and Illustrator
New York: North-South. 1996. 1-55858-575-3.

A young wolf loves to help his father with gardening chores in this lively text. Even though the help sometimes causes more work, the father encourages his son to help out so that he can learn how to work in the yard.

📖 *Book Extender:* This book provides students with an opportunity to join in the reading as it has a repetitive, rhyming phrase that builds throughout the text. Invite students to chime in when you point to the italic print.

This book can also be used to generate a discussion about different jobs students do around their house to contribute to their families and which jobs they can better complete now as a result of doing them more than once. The importance of trying and practicing to get better at any desired task can also be highlighted.

The Cat Barked?
Lydia Monks, Author and Illustrator
New York: Dial. 1998. 0-8037-2338-5.

"Be happy with who you are" is the message of this text. The cat thinks that it would be better to be a dog but after thinking through the pros and cons decides that being a cat is best.

🎺 *Focus on Phonological Awareness (phoneme blending):* Using some of the rhyming word pairs from the text, say the first word in the pair and break apart the second word, asking students to blend the sounds together to make the word that rhymes with the first word provided.

The Caterpillow Fight
Sam McBratney, Author
Jill Barton, Illustrator
Cambridge, MA: Candlewick. 1996. 1-56402-804-6.

What do caterpillars have when they are supposed to go to bed but want to have some fun instead? A caterpillow fight, of course! Children will join the fun as they hear about the rowdy pillow fight among the caterpillars and remember their own pillow fight experiences.

Christmas for Ten
Cathryn Falwell, Author and Illustrator
New York: Clarion. 1998. 0-395-85581-0.

Many preparations must be made to get ready for Christmas. This story shows how all family members contribute, making the preparations part of the celebration. From one to ten and then counting again, children are sure to relate to the many activities told with rhyming text.

📖 *Book Extender:* Invite children to tell of experiences they have with their families. This book is also good for sequencing. Have students recall what the family does first, second, and so on.

Chugga-Chugga-Choo
Kevin Lewis, Author
Daniel Kirk, Illustrator
New York: Hyperion. 1999. 078682379–8.

Here's a rhyming story that tells about a day in the life of a freight train. Come aboard the train and experience what the train experiences from sunup to sundown.

🎺 *Focus on Phonological Awareness:* The manner in which the text is written is perfect for showing how sounds can be stretched. Have them pretend to be the train by making the WHOOOOOO sounds as shown on the various pages.

Clara Ann Cookie
Harriet Ziefert, Author
Emily Bolam, Illustrator
Boston: Houghton Mifflin. 1999. 0-395-92324-7.

As many parents know, sometimes a backdoor approach is needed to help children complete a given activity without rebellion. Such is the case in this text. Clara's mother encourages her to make mean and ugly faces in the mirror while she is getting dressed to make Clara and herself less distressed. By the time she is dressed, Clara's grouchy mood changes to a pleasant one.

 Focus on Phonological Awareness (rhyming): To focus on rhyming words used in the book, tell students that you need them to take on the role of Clara. You will say two words. If they rhyme, they are to make a pleasant face; if they don't rhyme, make a mean, ugly face.

Clickety Clack
Rob and Amy Spence, Authors
Margaret Spengler, Illustrator
New York: Viking. 1999. 0-670-87946-0.

What happens when many different kinds and numbers of animals decide that they want to ride the train? In this book, the weight of all the animals causes the train to groan noisily. Of course, the animals themselves also cause quite a bit of noise. Children are sure to want to board the train disguised as different animals so that they can join in the fun.

 Focus on Phonological Awareness: Much initial consonant substitution makes this a perfect book to use for phoneme substitution. Using rhyming words from the text, create statements such as the following to use with children: "Take the /s/ off of *sack* and add some new sounds to *-ack* to make the word that tells where the train went." (*track*)

📖 *Book Extender:* Story dramatization is a logical follow-up to this book. Using paper strips, construct train tracks. Then have children take on the roles of different animals and board the train as you reread the story and they hear their animal name mentioned.

Cloud Cuckoo Land
Bernard Lodge, Author and Illustrator
Boston: Houghton Mifflin. 1999. 0-395-96318-4.

Take a trip to Cloud Cuckoo Land and other fun places in this text. Rhyming is used to create the verses used to take the various excursions that are sure to cause a giggle or two.

📖 *Book Extender:* Brainstorm with children other imaginary places the class could visit. Then, using the text as a sample, create a class verse to go with one of their imaginary places.

Color Crunch!
Charles Reasoner, Author and Illustrator
New York: Price/Stern/Sloan. 1996. 0-8431-3936-6.

Eat your way through colors—yes, you can, at least in this text. Rhyming verses are used to teach children about colors and the foods associated with them.

📖 *Book Extender:* Make a fruit salad with children bringing in fruits of different colors. Once all ingredients have been combined, feast on the colorful fruit salad. Also, you could have children go through their cold lunches and identify the colors of foods that they see.

Counting Crocodiles
Judy Sierra, Author
Will Hillenbrand, Illustrator
San Diego: Gulliver/Harcourt. 1997. 0-15-200192-1.

Have you ever eaten so much of one food that you got sick and tired of it? Well, this is exactly what happens to the monkey in this story. She eats so many lemons that she gets puckered up from the inside out. She spies another island that shows another food, but there's one problem: she has to get by the crocodiles. The story tells how she does just that, fooling them along the way with her cleverness and ability to count.

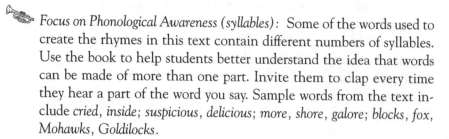 *Focus on Phonological Awareness (syllables):* Some of the words used to create the rhymes in this text contain different numbers of syllables. Use the book to help students better understand the idea that words can be made of more than one part. Invite them to clap every time they hear a part of the word you say. Sample words from the text include *cried, inside; suspicious, delicious; more, shore, galore; blocks, fox, Mohawks, Goldilocks.*

Cowboy Bunnies
Christine Loomis, Author
Ora Eitan, Illustrator
New York: Putnam. 1997. 0-399-22625-7.

In this text, little bunnies do what many children do: pretend to be something else. The bunnies pretend to be cowboys—riding their ponies, doing cowboy chores, and singing cowboy songs.

Cows Can't Fly
David Milgrim, Author and Illustrator
New York: Viking. 1998. 0-670-87475-2.

To young children, anything can be possible and such is the case in this story. Even though the boy in the story knows that cows can't fly, he decides to use his imagination and create a picture of cows flying through the air. His unsuccessful attempts to convince others that cows can fly lead him to the conclusion that only he can see the cows soaring through the air.

🎺 *Focus on Phonological Awareness (rhyming):* Play "fly away"! Tell students that you will say some words from the book, and if all of the words in the set rhyme, they are to say, "Fly away!" Sample words from the book include *sky, fly; me, see; downtown, down; fat, that; cow, now; dad, mad; away, say.*

📖 *Book Extender:* This book encourages children to use their imaginations. Invite them to think of other everyday objects and to use their imagination to create a picture and/or story about the adventures of the object.

Cows in the Kitchen
June Crebbin, Author
Katharine McEwen, Illustrator
Cambridge, MA: Candlewick. 0-7636-0645-6.

What do farm animals do when the farmer takes a nap? In this text, they go into the house and make quite a mess! Told in rhyme with the recurrent repetitive refrain, "That's what we do, Tom Farmer!", this text invites all readers to join in the fun as the animals make a mess of things and get shooed away from the house—only to return to wake up the farmer.

 Focus on Phonological Awareness (playing with sounds): Encourage students to take on the role of different animals and make the specific animal sounds when it's their turn. Doing so will build an awareness of different sounds and how the mouth feels when they are made.

📖 *Book Extender:* This book lends itself to shared reading in which the teacher reads the verse and the students chime in with "That's what we do, Tom Farmer!" Because of the repetition, students will have a successful choral reading experience as well.

Dancin' in the Kitchen
Wendy Gelsanliter and Frank Christian, Authors
Marjorie Priceman, Illustrator
New York: Putnam. 1998. 0-399-23035-1.

In this movin' story, three generations of a family work together to prepare a feast for all at Grandma's house. Inspired to move to the music on the kitchen radio, the family members work up quite an appetite while the dinner cooks. Once they finish eating, the dancing resumes as all pitch in to clean up.

 Focus on Phonological Awareness (blending): Using words from the text, invite children to blend sounds to tell you the word you are thinking of. For example, "I'm thinking of a word that tells what the family had to do while dinner was cooking. It has these sounds, /w/ /ā/ /t/. What's the word?" (*wait*)

📖 *Book Extender:* Each family member prepares a different part of the meal. Have students play match-up. Write each family member's name on a card and what they prepared on other cards. Distribute the cards to different class members and have them pair up by matching the family member with the appropriate activity. Display all of the paired cards in a pocket holder and reread the text to verify information.

Day by Day
Carol Shields, Author
True Kelley, Illustrator
New York: Dutton. 1998. 0-525-45457-8.

What do you do on different days of the week? Using rhymes, Shields provides listeners and readers with several activities for each day of the week. Youngsters are sure to delight in discovering how they and the characters in this book are alike through the activities they perform.

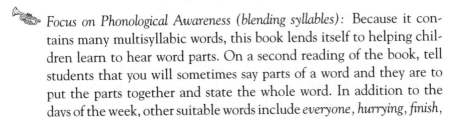 *Focus on Phonological Awareness (blending syllables):* Because it contains many multisyllabic words, this book lends itself to helping children learn to hear word parts. On a second reading of the book, tell students that you will sometimes say parts of a word and they are to put the parts together and state the whole word. In addition to the days of the week, other suitable words include *everyone, hurrying, finish, breakfast, button, ready, groceries, crackers, apples, shopping, library, teddy, sliding, wiggly,* and *funnies.*

📖 *Book Extender:* Invite children to tell about the activities they complete on each day of the week. After discussing these, children could also be encouraged to make an oral rhyme about one of the activities they mention. These could also be written down either by the teacher or by the students.

Elephants on Board
Suse MacDonald, Author and Illustrator
San Diego: Gulliver/Harcourt. 1999. 0-15-200951-5.

Several elephant performers are on their way to the circus but get a flat tire along the way. Different trucks arrive to help the elephants so that they don't miss their show. Tom's Trucking saves the day, providing the perfect vehicle to get all elephants to the circus.

📖 *Book Extender:* Digital times are provided as part of the rhyming text, making this a perfect book for helping students better understand clocks. On a second reading of the book, show them the digital time provided in the book, and, using a play clock with hands, show them how this time looks on a clock.

Edward the Emu
Sheena Knowles, Author
Rod Clement, Illustrator
New York: HarperTrophy. 1998. 0-06-44399-0.

Edward is tired of being an emu, so he decides to try on a new identity. He discovers the hard way that an emu is the best animal to be, all things considered. He returns to his pen and discovers a big surprise—a new emu whose name is Edwina!

📖 *Book Extender:* Like Edward, children may feel they would like to be somebody else. Have them tell about who they would like to be and why. This is also an excellent book for pantomime. Have children mimic the actions of the animals that Edward mimicked throughout the story.

Edwina the Emu
Sheena Knowles, Author
Rod Clement, Illustrator
New York: HarperTrophy. 1997. 0-06-443483-4.

Edwina shares with Edward that she has laid ten eggs. This news throws Edward for a loop as he tries to figure out how he will support ten chicks. Edwina comforts him by telling him that he can sit on the nest and she'll find a job, which is exactly what she does. In fact, her perfect job lands her right on the top of her nest!

🎺 *Focus on Phonological Awareness (rhyme):* Using rhyming words from the text, ask students to provide you with a word that the author used to rhyme with the one that you state. For example, "Give me the word that rhymes with zoo." (two) Sample words from the story include *zoo, two; fight, night; legs, eggs; street, feet; last, fast.*

Farmer Nat
Chris Demarest, Author and Illustrator
San Diego: Red Wagon/Harcourt. 1998. 0-15-200113-1.

Lift the flaps in this book and you'll discover who is making all the noise! This text informs readers of the different animals that live on a farm and the sound each makes. The book invites participation as readers/listeners must lift the flaps to reveal several animals. Told in simple, rhyming text, this book will help students develop an ear for rhyming words while simultaneously teaching them about animals.

📖 *Book Extender:* This is an excellent book to use for helping students make predictions. Have them examine the picture and state their predictions based on what they see. Lift the flap to confirm their predictions.

"Fire! Fire!" Said Mrs. McGuire
Bill Martin Jr., Author
Richard Egielski, Illustrator
San Diego: Harcourt. 1996. 0-15-227562-2.

The story is the same as when the book was first published in 1971—a chain of events that leads others to search out where a fire is located, only to discover that the source of the smoke is the candles of a birthday cake. What's changed are the illustrations, which provide different portrayals of the characters looking for the fire.

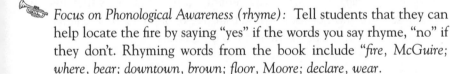 *Focus on Phonological Awareness (rhyme):* Tell students that they can help locate the fire by saying "yes" if the words you say rhyme, "no" if they don't. Rhyming words from the book include "*fire, McGuire; where, bear; downtown, brown; floor, Moore; declare, wear.*"

📖 *Book Extender:* This is an excellent book to use for chain of events. In fact, each character's name could be written on a long strip of paper, and as students retell the story, they could "chain" themselves together, showing the progression as stated in the book.

Five Little Kittens
Nancy Jewell, Author
Elizabeth Sayles, Illustrator
New York: Clarion. 1999. 0-395-77517-5.

In this rhyme, five little kittens are cared for by their mother and participate in many activities throughout their day. From sunup to sundown, the
five little kittens wear themselves out!

Follow Me!
Bethany Roberts, Author
Diane Greenseid, Illustrator
New York: Clarion. 1998. 0-395-82268-8.

Discover many creatures of the underwater world in this book! A mother
octopus leads her children through the water to meet various sea creatures. They enjoy meeting all of the animals with the exception of the eel,
who causes them to swim and hide in various places to escape being
devoured.

Focus on Phonological Awareness (rhyme): Create a rhyming ocean with
the class. Provide pictures of the different creatures and other objects
mentioned in the book. Show each pair, naming each object. If the
pair rhyme, have students place them in the rhyming ocean (a large
sheet of blue poster paper placed on the floor). Sample words from the
book include *weeds, reeds; fish, swish; sway, play; ink, sink; soar, floor;
zip, ship; wall, all.*

Book Extender: Have students generate a list of animals that live in
the sea and another list of those that live on land. Compare and contrast by pointing out likenesses and differences.

Four and Twenty Dinosaurs
Bernard Most, Author and Illustrator
San Diego: Voyager/Harcourt. 1999. 0-15-201959-6.

Traditional nursery rhymes are used to create the dinosaur rhymes in this
text. As they listen to this collection, children will note similarities with
the traditional rhymes as well as how Most innovated on the rhyme.

Book Extender: This book is a perfect example of how innovations
can be used to create stories based on a given pattern. Create some additional rhymes with students using the same pattern as Most. That is,

use most of the traditional rhyme but modify it to fit the creatures the students want to add.

From Anne to Zach
Mary Jane Martin, Author
Michael Grejniec, Illustrator
Honesdale, PA: Boyds Mills. 1996. 1-56397-573-4.

Letters of the alphabet are used to create many words, including those that are most meaningful to children — their names. In this book, children are exposed to the letters of the alphabet through children's names that start with each one. Through simple, rhyming verse, students join in the fun as they learn more about letters of the alphabet.

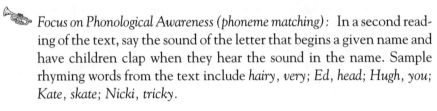 *Focus on Phonological Awareness (phoneme matching):* In a second reading of the text, say the sound of the letter that begins a given name and have children clap when they hear the sound in the name. Sample rhyming words from the text include *hairy, very; Ed, head; Hugh, you; Kate, skate; Nicki, tricky.*

📖 *Book Extender:* Have children introduce themselves using the same pattern as stated in the text (_____ my name is _____) and tell one thing they like to do. They could also write this sentence and provide an illustration of themselves doing one of their favorite activities or showing something about themselves.

Frozen Noses
Jan Carr, Author
Dorothy Donohue, Illustrator
New York: Holiday House. 1999. 0-8234-1462-0.

The children in this story are like many children: they love to play in the snow! Through simple rhyming text, children will discover many experiences in common with the story characters.

Gold Fever
Verla Kay, Author
S. D. Schindler, Illustrator
New York: Putnam. 1999. 0-399-23027-0.

Here's a brief glimpse of the gold rush that happened years ago. In rhyming text, this is the story of a farmer who did what so many others did during the gold rush: they left their families in search of the gold. In this case, Jasper leaves his farm and family thinking that digging for gold might be a bit easier than farming. He learns all too soon that mining for gold is as hard, if not harder, than farming, and he gladly returns home to his farm and family.

Grandma's Cat
Helen Ketteman, Author
Marsha Lynn Winborn, Illustrator
Boston: Houghton Mifflin. 1996. 0-395-73094-5.

As most cat lovers know, cats have a personality of their own and they only like to be bothered when they want to be bothered. The little girl in this story learns this lesson by paying attention to her grandmother's cat when she does not want to be bothered. The little girl finally wins over the cat, however, with her grandmother's help.

 Focus on Phonological Awareness (rhyme): Using a large grocery bag, construct a cat. Say two words from the text. If they rhyme, have students feed the cat by dropping dry cat food into the bag. Sample words from the text include *fat, cat; seek, peek; tree, knee; stair, there; clap, lap; burrs, purrs; bed, head.*

The Great Divide
Dale Ann Dodds, Author
Tracy Mitchell, Illustrator
Cambridge, MA: Candlewick. 1999. 0-7636-0442-9.

Eighty racers are determined to win a race that will take them across the country. Although they face some challenges along the way, one of the eighty racers crosses the finish line, winning the race. Rhyme and rhythm make this an engaging book.

Greetings, Sun
Phillis and David Gershator, Authors
Synthia Saint James, Illustrator
New York: DK. 1998. 0-7894-2482-7.

Using simple rhythmic and repetitive text, this book helps children greet many different objects that they encounter throughout the day. Beginning with greeting the sun and ending with greeting the moon, the children see that there are many things to greet in any given day.

The Grumpy Morning
Pamela Edwards, Author
Darcia Labrosse, Illustrator
New York: Hyperion. 1998. 0-7868-2279-1.

The cow needs to be attended to, and with one "moo," she sets off a chain reaction in which all the other animals tell the farmer, each in its own unique way, that they need some attention, too! All of this complaining awakens the farmer, who takes care of the animals' needs, one by one.

 Focus on Phonological Awareness (initial substitution, phoneme manipulation): After reading through the book one time, reread the book stopping at the end of every second line to provide students with time to fill in the rhyming word. Then ask them questions such as "What did we take away from 'moo' to make the word 'do'?"

Guess Who's Coming, Jesse Bear
Nancy White Carlstrom, Author
Bruce Degen, Illustrator
New York: Simon & Schuster. 1998. 0-689-80702-3.

Jesse Bear discovers that one of his least favorite cousins is coming for a visit. Counting the days until her arrival, Jesse dreads the final moment. However, as the week progresses, Jesse and his cousin Sara get along quite well, and in the end, he discovers that he will miss Sara when she leaves.

Here Comes Mother Goose
Iona Opie, Editor
Rosemary Wells, Illustrator
Cambridge, MA: Candlewick. 1999. 0-7636-0683-9.

In this collection of over sixty familiar nursery rhymes, every character takes on a different look due to Wells' illustrations. Large print, lots of space, and colorful illustrations make this book an excellent choice for a read-aloud collection.

Hippos Go Berserk!
Sandra Boynton, Author and Illustrator
New York: Aladdin. 1996. 0-689-80818-6.

One hippo decides that he is lonely so he calls to invite another over. He, in turn, calls others and so on, so that many guests show up in increasingly larger numbers. An all-night party ensues, and the guests gradually depart the following morning.

Focus on Phonological Awareness (rhyme): Another way for the hippos to go berserk is to hear words that don't rhyme. Say two words from the book, telling students that the hippos will go berserk if the words don't rhyme. If they do not rhyme, students say "Hippos go berserk!" Sample rhyming words from the book include *alone, phone; door, four; overdressed, guest; forth, north; say, day, way.*

Book Extender: Use this book to help children better understand ordinal numbers. Ask students to state who came first, second, and so on.

The House Book
Keith DuQuette, Author and Illustrator
New York: Putnam. 1999. 0-399-23183-8.

Students will learn many parts to a house as a result of listening to this rhyming text. From start to finish, DuQuette uses simple rhyming text to explain how houses are constructed.

Book Extender: To further students' understanding of mapping skills, encourage them to make a floor plan of their own house or apartment. The floor plan provided in the text can serve as an example.

How Do You Say It Today, Jesse Bear?
Nancy White Carlstrom, Author
Bruce Degen, Illustrator
New York: Aladdin. 1999. 0-689-82424-6.

From January to December, Jesse Bear completes many activities. This book shares those he completes for each month of the year. Simple rhyming text is used to engage readers and listeners.

📖 *Book Extender:* To help children better understand the months of the year, have them create their own monthly activity books. To prevent students from becoming overwhelmed, have this be an ongoing activity throughout the school year. On the last day of the month, provide children with time to draw or find pictures of things that they did in the month and to affix these to the appropriate page in their "Months of the Year" books.

The Hullabaloo ABC
Beverly Cleary, Author
Ted Rand, Illustrator
New York: Morrow. 1998. 0-688-15182-5.

Morning on the farm brings anything but silence as this book well illustrates! Three children make or hear noises for every letter of the alphabet as they run about the farm. From A for *Aha!* to Z for *zoom*, listeners and readers experience the farm in a very noisy way through simple rhyming verse. The watercolor illustrations add to the fun by showing just who is making all the noise.

I Spy: An Alphabet in Art
Lucy Micklethwait, Compiler
New York: Mulberry. 1996. 0-688-14730-5.

Famous paintings and rhyming, repetitive verses are used to help children learn the letters of the alphabet. Each verse begins with "I spy with my little eye something beginning with _____." Opposite the verse is a full-page famous painting that has at least one object that begins with the given letter. The name of the painting and the artist are provided at the bottom of each verse.

🎺 *Focus on Phonological Awareness (phoneme matching):* Have children play the I spy game. After listening to the book, have them name objects they spy around the room that begin with a given sound. Say

something such as, "I spy with my little eye something beginning with
_____." However, instead of stating the name of the letter,
provide the sound.

I Spy Spooky Night: A Book of Picture Riddles
Jean Marzollo, Author
Walter Wick, Illustrator
New York: Scholastic. 1996. 0-590-48137-1.

This book comprises thirteen picture riddles, each inviting exploration.
After reading or listening to the rhyming verse, listeners and readers can
look closely at the accompanying picture to locate items mentioned in the
verse. Additional "extra credit riddles" are listed in the back of the book,
providing students with additional searching opportunities.

📖 *Book Extender:* Invite students to draw pictures and make up an accompanying riddle. Assemble these in your class collection of "I Spy"
picture riddles.

I Swapped My Dog
Harriet Ziefert, Author
Emily Bolam, Illustrator
Boston: Houghton Mifflin. 1998. 0-395-89159-0.

In this circular tale, a farmer makes several trades only to end up with what
he started—his dog! Along with all this trading, the farmer discovers that
different animals will provide different kinds of experiences and that no
one animal is perfect. The message? Be happy with what you have!

📖 *Book Extender:* To teach children about circular plots, draw a large
circle on the board. Have children trace the steps that led the man
back to his dog, making notations on the outer edge of the circle along
the way.

In the Small, Small Pond
Denise Fleming, Author and Illustrator
New York: Holt. 1998. 0-8050-5983-0.

This Caldecott honor book tells and shows the many animals and insects that live on and in a freshwater pond. From spring to fall, simple rhyming text is used to tell of the many activities in which these creatures engage.

 Focus on Phonological Awareness (phoneme substitution): During a second reading of the book, invite children to create new words just like the author did. For example, you might say, "If I take away the /w/ in *wiggle* and put /j/ in its place, what word will I have?" (*jiggle*)

Iron Horses
Verla Kay, Author
Michael McCurdy, Illustrator
New York: Putnam. 1999. 0-399-23119-6.

Here is the story of how the railroad was built across the United States. Told with simple rhyming text, the few words convey major historical information about the construction of the railroad. The book closes with an author's note and a map that shows where the railroad was constructed—from Sacramento, California, to Omaha, Nebraska, and vice versa.

It's About Time, Jesse Bear, and Other Rhymes
Nancy White Carlstrom, Author
Bruce Degen, Illustrator
New York: Aladdin. 1998. 0-689-81849-1.

This is a compilation of rhymes that tell about the many activities Jesse Bear completes throughout a day. Rhymes are provided for just about every activity—from getting dressed to getting ready for bed.

📖 *Book Extender:* These poems could serve as an excellent resource for choral reading. Enlarge each and invite students to share in the reading.

Jump!
Steve Lavis, Author and Illustrator
New York: Lodestar. 1997. 0-525-67578-7.

A little boy, a teddy bear, and a frog perform several actions with other animals. The story is told in simple rhythmic verse. Listeners will be eager to join in the fun by imitating the actions and repeating the catchy refrains.

📖 *Book Extender:* This book lends itself to classroom drama. Encourage students to take on the roles of the various animals and perform the same actions. Every child in the class could perform every role, or students could select which animal they would like to be. Have students perform the actions in the order the animals appear in the text.

Kangaroo and Cricket
Lorianne Siomades, Author and Illustrator
Honesdale, PA: Boyds Mills. 1999. 1-56397-780-X.

Here is a book of opposites to help children better understand this concept. Children also learn how they are alike and different from one another as a result of the opposites used in the book.

🎺 *Focus on Phonological Awareness (rhyme):* Tell children that one way some of the animals in the book can be alike is by having something in common. Today, what they have in common is words that rhyme. Then ask students questions such as the following: "How are *kangaroo* and *cricket* like *camel* and *turtle?*" (Kangaroo and turtle *jump*; camel and turtle have a *hump*.)

Knock at the Door and Other Baby Action Rhymes
Kay Chorao, Author and Illustrator
New York: Dutton. 1999. 0-525-45969-3.

Twenty action rhymes are assembled here to engage students in much language play. Each rhyme is accompanied by diagrams to show the specific hand and body movements that can be used to tell the rhyme.

Let's Go Visiting
Sue Williams, Author
Julie Vivas, Illustrator
San Diego: Harcourt. 1998. 0-15-201823-9.

Here is a counting story in which a young boy visits his farmyard friends to see if they are ready to play. As different animals are visited, they join the boy as he visits the succeeding animals. Both the visiting and the playing tire him and his friends out, causing them to curl up for a sleep.

📖 *Book Extender*: This book is a natural for shared reading. As one reader reads the part of the new animal, the rest can chime in with the repeated refrain, "Let's go visiting. What do you say?" To reinforce the concept of sequencing story events, have students volunteer to be the different animals and stand in order to show when they appeared in the text.

Little Fish, Lost
Nancy Van Laan, Author
Jane Conteh-Morgan, Illustrator
New York: Atheneum. 1998. 0-689-81331-7.

Little Fish is in search of his mother, and in his search he discovers several animals in an African pond along the way. He is finally reunited with his mother after swimming through reeds.

 Focus on Phonological Awareness (phoneme manipulation): Many of the rhyming words in this text are created by adding or deleting phonemes. Questions such as the following can be used to focus children's attention on this phoneme manipulation:

1. What sound is added to lap to make *slap*?
2. Take away the /s/ and add /k/ and what's the word? (*clap*)
3. Take way the /k l/ and add /sn/. What's the word? (*snap*)
4. What sound do we take away from *snappa* to make *snap*? *digga* to make *dig*? *zigga* to make *zig*?

📖 *Book Extender*: Have students take on the roles of the different animals that Little Fish encounters as he looks for his mother. After they are standing in order, ask one student to take on the role of Little Fish, swimming by each and making the same movements as stated in the text. The students taking on the roles of animals should do the same (e.g., Beetle scooped a tunnel).

Little Red Monkey
Jonathan London, Author
Frank Remkiewicz, Illustrator
New York: Dutton. 1997. 0-525-45642-2.

This is no ordinary monkey! This one likes to dance in his underpants! In the jungle and all the way to Timbuktu, Little Red Monkey knows just where to stop to perform a dance. The text is sure to entice children to do their own dances.

Little White Dog
Laura Godwin, Author
Dan Yaccarino, Illustrator
New York: Hyperion. 1998. 0-7868-2256.

Several animals disappear in the background as the story progresses. Once the lights are turned on, however, each animal searches and finds the succeeding animal until they are all discovered by the end of the text.

📖 *Book Extender:* This is another excellent book for helping students better understand sequencing events in a story. Ask for volunteers to represent the various animals shown in the text. In keeping with the text, have these children "disappear" and return when mentioned in the text. To turn on the light, as in the text, one student needs to be given a flashlight or instructed to turn on the lights as the signal to the other animals to begin returning from their hiding places.

Look-Alikes
Joan Steiner, Author and Illustrator
New York: Little, Brown. 1998. 0-316-81255-2.

Using simple verses, Steiner invites listeners or readers to identify commonplace objects that are used to construct the eleven scenes she presents in this book. In this land of look-alikes, the more you look, the more you'll see! The vivid illustrations and photographs are captivating from start to finish. Answers and additional challenges are provided at the end of the book. Little, Brown also publishes the sequel to this book, which is entitled *Look-Alikes Jr.* (1999. ISBN: 0-316-81307-9).

The Low-Down Laundry Line Blues
C. M. Millen, Author
Christine Davenier, Illustrator
Boston: Houghton Mifflin. 1999. 0-395-87497-1.

Have you ever felt sorry for yourself, enjoying all the wallowing in self-pity, only to have someone come along and snap you out of it? This is exactly what happens in this text as an older sister mopes and her younger sister does everything within her power to cheer her up. Jump rope finally does the trick!

📖 *Book Extender:* Talking with students about moods and emotions is a natural extension of this text. Provide time for students to tell about what makes them happy, sad, and the like.

Mad Summer Night's Dream
Ruth Brown, Author and Illustrator
New York: Dutton. 1999. 0-525-46010-1.

As we all know, many things can happen in dreams. In this young girl's dream, birds blossom and flowers sing, among other strange events. Anything is possible until, of course, we awaken only to discover that it was all a dream. Children will take pleasure in learning about the different happenings in the dream portrayed in this book.

Madison Finds a Line
Sunny Warner, Author and Illustrator
Boston: Houghton Mifflin. 1999. 0-395-88508-6.

Follow a line in your own backyard and what will you discover? In this book, the answer is a concert being performed by some bug musicians. Join in the fun as Madison and her cat dance and sing their way through the many challenges in their adventure.

Mice Squeak, We Speak
Tomie dePaola, Author and Illustrator
New York: Putnam. 1997. 0-399-23202-8.

How do animals communicate? The words in this text answer this question. Through simple rhymes accompanied by supportive illustrations, children learn the sounds that different animals make.

 Focus on Phonological Awareness (rhyme): Say rhyming words from the text and tell students to say "yes" if they rhyme and "no" if they don't. Sample words include *roar, snore; creak, squeak, speak; squawk, talk.*

Millions of Snowflakes
Mary McKenna Siddals, Author
Elizabeth Sayles, Illustrator
New York: Clarion. 19980-395-71531-8.

Most children will relate to the rhyming verse in this book. A little girl counts snowflakes as they fall on different parts of her body. She also plays in the snow as the flakes fall around and on her.

📖 *Book Extender:* This book lends itself well to children talking about their adventures in the snow. After they share, transfer their spoken language to written form by constructing a list of activities to do in the snow. Of course, this activity will be even more meaningful if it is snowing and children have just come in from playing outside.

Miss Bindergarten Celebrates the 100th Day of Kindergarten
Joseph Slate, Author
Ashley Wolf, Illustrator
New York: Dutton. 1998. 0-525-4600-4.

To celebrate the 100th day of kindergarten, Miss Bindergarten has instructed her students (whose names begin with A through Z) to bring 100 of something from home. As this rhythmic, rhyming story unfolds, we get a glimpse of what the children do as they complete this homework assignment as well as what Miss Bindergarten does behind the scenes to make the most of the day. The book closes with a two-page spread showing what each student brought.

📖 *Book Extender:* Use the last two pages to provide students with an opportunity to learn how to summarize and retell. The book can also be used to help students better understand sequencing. Write each of

Miss Bindergarten's students names and what they brought on a card. Invite students to place them in the packet holder in the same order as in the text. Have one student in class cross-check with the book. Puzzles can also be created by putting the name of a student mentioned in the story on one part of a card and what the student brought on another. Distribute the pieces and have students pair up according to what each one of Miss Bindergarten's students brought.

Miss Spider's New Car
David Kirk, Author and Illustrator
New York: Scholastic. 1997. 0-590-30713-4.

Miss Spider decides that she needs to buy a new car so that she can have a safe journey to visit her mother, and this is where the fun begins! She tries out several cars, each providing a different kind of ride. At long last, she finds the perfect car, which she thinks she will use to visit her mother. However, her mother writes her another message. Read to discover just what it is!

Monkey Do!
Allan Ahlberg, Author
André Amstutz, Illustrator
Cambridge, MA: Candlewick. 1998. 0-7636-0466-6.

A clever monkey escapes from his cage in the zoo and explores the world beyond in this rhythmic tale. As much as he enjoys meeting others, however, he decides that he needs to return to the zoo because he misses his mother.

Focus on Phonological Awareness (rhyme): Tell students that you will say a set of words used in the book. One of the words will not rhyme with the others. They must listen to all the words and tell you which one does not rhyme with the other two. For example, you might say something like, "Zoo, do, feet. Which one does not rhyme?" Other words from the book that can be used for this activity include *street, feet; Sam, scram; blue, chew, too, stew; road, load.*

Book Extender: A logical extension of this book involves students in a discussion about the monkey's journey—who he met first, second, and so on. Invite children to share in the reading by chiming in with "Monkey see, monkey do" when directed to do so during a second or third reading of the text.

Monster Math
Anne Miranda, Author
Polly Powell, Illustrator
San Diego: Harcourt. 1999. 0-15-201835-2.

What could be more fun than inviting several friends to a birthday party? That's exactly how Monster feels about its birthday as several groups of monsters arrive to join in the fun, causing the party to get a little out of control. After a full day of fun, the monsters leave one grateful and glad monster behind exclaiming that this is the best birthday ever! Its exhausted mother agrees!

📖 *Book Extender:* This book also focuses on counting through ten as well as counting by tens. Therefore, it can be used to introduce or reinforce how to count by tens.

Month by Month a Year Goes Round
Carol Shields, Author
True Kelley, Illustrator
New York: Dutton. 1998. 0-525-45458-6.

Every month of the year brings change and different activities. This book highlights both. The simple rhymes are sure to help children relate to the many activities shown throughout the book.

🎺 *Focus on Phonological Awareness (phoneme matching: medial sounds):* Tell students that you will say a set of words from the text. Their job is to listen carefully and state which of the three words has a different sound in the middle:

Set 1: drip, *drop*, drip
Set 2: plip, *plop*, plip
Set 3: squish, *squash*, squish

Moondogs
Daniel Kirk, Author and Illustrator
New York: Putnam. 1999. 0-399-23128-5.

Sometimes the best things are right under our noses, and this is exactly what Willy Joe discovers. He thinks he wants a moondog but soon discovers that a regular earth dog can be a person's best friend.

The Movable Mother Goose
Robert Sabuda, Illustrator
New York: Little Simon. 1999. 0-689-81192-6.

Every nursery rhyme comes to life in this pop-up book. The creatures' names in the rhyme literally unfold as the page or door telling the rhyme opens. Children are sure to like the action behind each of these rhymes.

Mouse Creeps
Peter Harris, Author
Reg Cartwright, Illustrator
New York: Dial. 1997. 0-8037-2183-8.

It all begins with a mouse who sets off a chain of events that lead to the end of a war—something not foreseen at the onset. Through a domino effect, youngsters see that the influence of one creature can have a dramatic effect on others. The message? One person *can* make a difference!

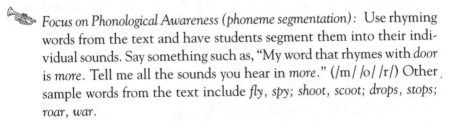 *Focus on Phonological Awareness (phoneme segmentation):* Use rhyming words from the text and have students segment them into their individual sounds. Say something such as, "My word that rhymes with *door* is *more*. Tell me all the sounds you hear in *more*." (/m/ /o/ /r/) Other sample words from the text include *fly, spy; shoot, scoot; drops, stops; roar, war.*

📖 *Book Extender:* This tale is cyclical, leading us right back to the beginning by ending with the same lines. Invite students to use this same story structure to tell of another adventure that includes a series of events beginning with "Dog sleeps. Mouse creeps."

Mouse Mess
Linnea Riley, Author and Illustrator
New York: Blue Sky/Scholastic. 1997. 0-590-10048-3.

When there's a mouse in the house, a mess is sure to follow. Such is the case in this book. He's not trying to make a mess; it happens as he is looking for just the right food to quench his appetite. Tummy full, he leaves a mess behind him.

Focus on Phonological Awareness (phoneme manipulation): Select words from the book that can be used to show how the author played with sounds to create new words. Sample words include *munch, crunch; cracker, snacker; flakes, makes.* Then invite students to do the same by saying something such as the following for the words you select: "Take away the /m/ in *munch.* Add /kr/. What's your new word?" (*crunch*)

My Box of Colors
Lorianne Siomades, Author and Illustrator
Honesdale, PA: Boyds Mills. 1998. 1-56397-711-7.

Valuing and celebrating our differences is what this rhyming book is all about. Through colors, the text encourages children to accept people, places, and things just as they are.

📖 *Book Extender:* Create different bar graphs to show students how they are alike and different. For example, create an eye bar graph by giving students small squares the same color as their eyes. In turn, have them place their squares in the right section on the bar graph.

My Crayons Talk
Patricia Hubbard, Author
G. Brian Karas, Illustrator
New York: Holt. 1996. 0-8050-3529-X.

If crayons could talk, what would they say? This book provides some answers as each one has something to say. As Brown sings, "Play, Mud-pie day," Pink laughs, "Clown! Pants fall down!" Youngsters will think of their crayons in a different way after experiencing this book.

Focus on Phonological Awareness (rhyme): Provide students with a set of rhyming words asking them to clap if the set rhymes. Sample words from the text include *yum, gum; play, day; chick, quick; wise, eyes; most, ghost; clown, down.*

📖 *Book Extender:* Invite students to create things that their crayons might say using a simple rhyme patterned after the text. They could also provide illustrations for their verse.

My Friend Bear
Jez Alborough, Author and Illustrator
Cambridge, MA: Candlewick. 1998. 0-7636-0583-2.

Ever feel sad and wish that you had a friend to talk to? Such is the case in this story of Eddie and the bear. Both want a friend and they just so happen to meet one another, becoming good friends regardless of their size!

My Puffer Train
Mary Murphy, Author and Illustrator
Boston: Houghton Mifflin. 1999. 0-395-97105-5.

A penguin decides to drive his train through the country and discovers several different kinds of animals along the way. All board his train for a fun ride.

 Focus on Phonological Awareness (phoneme isolation): Tell students to listen to the three words you will say and that you want them to tell you the sound at the beginning or end of all three words. For example, "Tell me the sound you hear at the beginning of these: *Puffa, puffa, puffa.*" Or "Tell me the sound you hear at the end of these words: *grump, grump, grump.*" Other words from the book include *thump, thump, thump; cheep, cheep, cheep; splish, splash, splosh.*

Night House Bright House
Monica Wellington, Author and Illustrator
New York: Dutton. 1997. 0-525-45491-8.

In every room of the house, ten mice keep activity stirred up throughout the evening while the objects in the house make their comments about the games going on around them. The text is filled with word play inviting children to join in the fun.

 Focus on Phonological Awareness (phoneme substitution): This book is loaded with examples of words that are created by phoneme substitution. Each is accompanied by a rebus sentence. Example: "'Tickle-tickle,' said the pickle." Provide children with one set and ask how the first word was changed to create the second word.

No Matter What
Debi Gliori, Author and Illustrator
San Diego: Harcourt. 1999. 0-15-202061-6.

A little fox named Small seeks reassurance from his mother, Large, that she will always love him no matter what. By posing several possible scenarios, Small gradually realizes that Large will always love him and that love is a feeling that never wears out.

October Smiled Back
Lisa Westberg Peters, Author
Ed Young, Illustrator
New York: Holt. 1996. 0-8050-1776-3.

The months of the year are personified in this book. From shy November through October, who smiles, children experience the various feelings associated with friendship.

 Focus on Phonological Awareness (phoneme segmentation): Provide some practice with phoneme segmentation by providing children with a word used in the text and asking them to state every sound they hear.

📖 *Book Extender:* This book is perfect for encouraging students to talk about feelings that we all experience at different times and about how these feelings can be triggered by the seasons and weather conditions. Encourage children to talk about days that make them feel like doing specific activities.

One Duck, Stuck
Phyllis Root, Author
Jane Chapman, Illustrator
Cambridge, MA: Candlewick. 0-7636-0334-1.

One day a duck gets stuck in the sleepy, slimy marsh, and try as she might, she cannot get out. In turn, increasingly larger groups of animals work together to pull her out. From fish to moose, this rhyming, repetitive text sends the message that working together is valuable, as is helping someone in need.

 Focus on Phonological Awareness (rhyme): Invite students to detect differences in words that are used to create rhymes. For example, *pricky, sticky.* Ask them which sounds are the same and which are different.

📖 *Book Extender:* Divide the class into different parts, each taking on the role of the different animals who will help the duck. One group can also take on the role of the duck and read the refrain "Help! Help! Who can help?" at the appropriate times. Another group can chime in with the verse that tells what happened as a result of the animals' trying to help the duck. This book is also a counting book in that increasingly larger groups of animals try to help (e.g., two fish, three moose). Therefore, students could be grouped accordingly and could sit in numerical order when sharing their parts.

One of Each
Mary Ann Hoberman, Author
Marjorie Priceman, Illustrator
New York: Little, Brown. 1997. 0-316-36731-1.

Oliver Tolliver is a dog who lives alone in his house, and he has one of everything he needs. He is so proud of his house that he would like to show it to another. Gradually, Oliver discovers that sharing with others is much more fun than just having one of everything!

📖 *Book Extender:* This book is a perfect lead-in to talking with students about sharing with others and the enjoyment that is manifested as a result.

One Horse Waiting for Me
Patricia Mullins, Author and Illustrator
New York: Simon & Schuster. 1998. 0-689-81381-3.

This book is a must for children who enjoy horses. All types of horses are shown, most often performing different tasks. From 1 through 12, each rhythmic verse makes the book a pleasure to read aloud or enjoy on one's own.

One Monkey Too Many
Jackie French Koller, Author
Lynn Munsinger, Illustrator
San Diego: Harcourt. 1999. 0-15-200006-2.

The monkeys in this story simply want to have some fun. That's what vacations are for, aren't they? Well, fun they have, along with some unexpected adventures that begin when too many of them pile on a bike built for only one. Come join the fun, and you'll discover how too many monkeys ended up in this story!

Once I Was . . .
Niki Clark Leopold, Author
Woodleigh Marx Hubbard, Illustrator
New York: Putnam. 1999. 0-399-23105-6.

Change is a certainty, as this story well illustrates. Objects take on different forms, becoming different objects. For instance, an alphabet turns into a book, a penny into a sun. Discover other common objects that make transformations in this text.

📖 *Book Extender:* Have children use the basic idea presented in this book to create their own object transformations. Provide time for them to choose a picture from a magazine and use their crayons to turn the selected picture into another object. All of these could be collected and assembled into a book for the classroom library entitled *Our Transformations*.

Out to Lunch
Peggy Perry Anderson, Author and Illustrator
Boston: Houghton Mifflin. 1998. 0-395-89826-9.

Like many children, Joe has a difficult time sitting still and minding his manners when he goes out to lunch at a fancy restaurant with his parents. Try as they might, Joe's parents cannot seem to get Joe to obey, making the eating experience a miserable one for them as well as for every other person in the restaurant who comes into contact with them.

A Pig Tale
Olivia Newton-John and Brian Seth Hurst, Authors
Sal Murdocca, Illustrator
New York: Aladdin. 1999. 0-689-82428-9.

Here's the story of a packpig—a pig who saves everything, to the embarrassment of his own son. However, Iggy the packpig creates fantastic objects by recycling the material that looks like junk. Told with rhyming text, the message here is that we need to pay attention to our environment and its needs, too!

Focus on Phonological Awareness (rhyme): Each stanza in this story is written in four lines with the second and fourth lines ending in rhyming words. During a second reading of this book, read each stanza, pausing before you state the last word in the fourth line to provide students with an opportunity to fill in the missing rhyming word.

Book Extender: Provide children with an everyday object that some people view as trash—an egg carton, for example. Provide them with other supplies so that they can use the object to make a new creation and learn about the value of recycling along the way.

Quack and Count
Keith Baker, Author and Illustrator
San Diego: Harcourt. 1999. 0-15-292858-8.

There are many ways to count to seven, as the seven ducklings in this book discover. Through different activities and combinations of ducklings, different number sentences are provided, all of which add up to seven.

📖 *Book Extender:* Invite students to construct number sentences using manipulatives. They can state their sentences or write them down. Here's an example of an oral sentence stated as students actually use objects to tell it: "There are three ducks and four more meet them at the pond. There are seven ducks in all."

Quacky Quack-Quack
Ian Whybrow, Author
Russell Ayto, Illustrator
Cambridge, MA: Candlewick. 1998. 0-7636-0510-7.

What happens when you eat the bread that you were supposed to feed to the ducks? Chances are you raise quite a commotion, which is exactly what happens in this book when Baby Brother eats the bread. Luckily, Older Brother saves the day by giving the baby his ice cream cone in exchange for the bread, which he uses to feed the ducks and geese. All returns to normal with the baby joining in the feeding.

 Focus on Phonological Awareness: The way this book is written invites language play. When you come to enlarged print, invite students to make the sounds of the animals.

Pets!
Melrose Cooper, Author
Yumi Heo, Illustrator
New York: Holt. 1998. 0-8050-3893-0.

How can you choose just one pet when there are so many to choose from? After surveying all the pets at the pet show, a young child chooses one that he can hold — or does the pet hold the child?

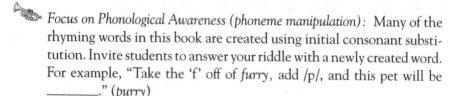 *Focus on Phonological Awareness (phoneme manipulation):* Many of the rhyming words in this book are created using initial consonant substitution. Invite students to answer your riddle with a newly created word. For example, "Take the 'f' off of *furry*, add /p/, and this pet will be _____." (*purry*)

📖 *Book Extender:* It seems as though all children long for a pet — some have them, some don't. This book lends itself to a discussion about the pets children have and those they might like to have.

Rush Hour
Christine Loomis, Author
Mari Takabayashi, Illustrator
Boston: Houghton Mifflin. 1996. 0-395-69129-X.

What is it like to live in a big city? This book provides a glimpse into the city to help answer this question. Beginning with the early morning and ending with coming home again at night, it shows how different people get ready for work and the mode of transportation they use to get there and back home again.

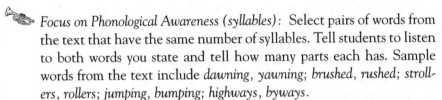 *Focus on Phonological Awareness (syllables):* Select pairs of words from the text that have the same number of syllables. Tell students to listen to both words you state and tell how many parts each has. Sample words from the text include *dawning, yawning; brushed, rushed; strollers, rollers; jumping, bumping; highways, byways.*

📖 *Book Extender:* A natural follow-up calls for time for children to talk about how they get to school and how their parents get to work. This discussion could lead into studying about modes of transportation. Children could compare or contrast modes of transportation where they live with those used in other places — the country, for example.

Safe, Warm, and Snug
Stephen R. Swinburne, Author
Jose Aruego and Ariane Dewey, Illustrators
San Diego: Gulliver/Harcourt. 1999. 0-15-201734-8.

Different animals protect their young from predators and the weather in different ways, which is what this book is all about. Discover how animals such as kangaroos and pythons ensure safety.

📖 *Book Extender:* This book can serve as a catalyst for learning about animals and how they protect their young. As discoveries are made, they can be written on the class chart for all to see.

Sleepy Bears
Mem Fox, Author
Kerry Argent, Illustrator
San Diego: Harcourt. 1999. 0-15-202016-0.

How does a mother convince her children that it is time to come inside and go to bed? In this story about six bears and their mother, the task is accomplished by telling each of them their very own story, which puts them to sleep for the winter.

 Focus on Phonological Awareness (phoneme blending): Because the word *fast* is written with several *a*'s to encourage the reader to stretch it out, this is an excellent book to use to point out to children how sounds can be stretched in words and then blended together to form a single word. Point out that the author is showing you how to say the word *fast* by writing it a certain way. Then show them the word in the text to help them make connections.

So Many Bunnies: A Bedtime ABC and Counting Book
Rick Walton, Author
Paige Miglio, Illustrator
New York: Lothrop. 1998. 0-688-13656-7.

The old mother rabbit that lives in this shoe has twenty-six bunnies, and she knows just what to do with each one of them! Through rhyming text, listeners and readers experience the entire alphabet of bunnies, beginning with Abel and ending with Zed, discovering the special sleeping places Mother Rabbit designates for each.

So Say the Little Monkeys
Nancy Van Laan, Author
Yumi Heo, Illustrator
New York: Atheneum. 1998. 0-689-81038-5.

This is the retelling of an Indian folktale from Brazil about small, playful monkeys. It explains why they have no home according to the Indians — they like to play more than anything else! The text is full of rhymes and words that invite youngsters to make the many sounds that the monkeys make.

📖 *Book Extender:* This story is somewhat cumulative in that the monkeys make different sounds and perform different actions on different days. The verse then incorporates the current sound and action along

68

with those completed on previous days. Students could be invited to dramatize the book by making the different motions or sounds the monkeys make—in the same sequence. Or different students could volunteer to perform different actions.

Sun Song
Jean Marzollo, Author
Laura Regan, Illustrator
New York: HarperTrophy. 1995. 0-06-443476-1.

We all respond to the sun in different ways. This book shows how different animals and plants respond to the daylight as it changes throughout the day. Four-line verses are used to tell the story.

Sunflower House
Eve Bunting, Author
Kathryn Hewitt, Illustrator
San Diego: Voyager/Harcourt. 1999. 0-15-201952-9.

In addition to using sunflowers to create a summer playhouse, the youngster in this story learns about the life cycle of the sunflower, from planting the seed to having the flower generate new seeds that can be used the following year to keep the cycle going. Children are sure to relate to the content of this text.

   📖 *Book Extender:* Provide each child with a plastic container, some dirt, and a sunflower seed and show him or her how to plant the seeds. Make sure that the seed is planted along the side of the plastic container so that they can actually watch it grow. Have children note their observations of their sunflower's growth in their "Scientist's Observation Log."

Sunrise
Helena Clare Pittman, Author
Michael Rex, Illustrator
San Diego: Silver Whistle/Harcourt. 1998. 0-15-201684-8.

Experience a counting rhyme that tells about the chaos a family experiences one morning. From sunrise until it's time to board the school bus, all members are involved in many activities. Every two-word sentence or phrase has one word that rhymes with *lies*. The colorful, bright illustrations bring the text to life.

Focus on Phonological Awareness (rhyme): During a second reading of the book, ask children to listen for all words that rhyme with *lies* and to clap when they hear one.

📖 *Book Extender:* Display the numbers one through ten and invite children to retell the story mentioning what was associated with each number in the text. Choose another student to be the "cross-checker" with the actual text.

Ten Little Bears: A Counting Rhyme
Kathleen Hague, Author
Michael Hague, Illustrator
New York: Morrow. 1999. 0-688-16383-1.

Ten bears have many different adventures as they play. Told in simple rhyming text, this book also provides an opportunity for youngsters to count backwards from ten.

Ten Terrible Dinosaurs
Paul Strickland, Author and Illustrator
New York: Dutton. 1997. 0-525-45905-7.

Here's a book about ten dinosaurs who romp and roar across the pages. One by one, they leave the scene until only one remains. He's just about asleep when the other nine appear and holler, "ROAR!"

Focus on Phonological Awareness (rhyme): Invite students to stand up if the two words you say rhyme and to stay seated if they don't. Sample words from the text include *line, nine; great, eight; heaven, seven; tricks, six; jive, five; floor, four.*

📖 *Book Extender:* This is an excellent book for teaching students something about subtraction. Provide ten manipulatives shaped like dinosaurs and display them in front of the students before beginning a second read of the book. As dinosaurs leave, take away one manipulative and have students count those that remain.

These Hands
Hope Lynne Price, Author
Bryan Collier, Illustrator
New York: Hyperion. 1999. 0-78682320-8.

What are the many things that hands can do? This book names quite a few! From touching to creating, this book celebrates hands.

Focus on Phonological Awareness (rhyme): Taking your lead from the book, have children trace their hands on a large sheet of paper. Then provide magazines and have children cut pictures that rhyme and glue them onto their traced hands.

To Market, To Market
Anne Miranda, Author
Janet Stevens, Illustrator
San Diego: Harcourt. 1997. 0-15-200035-6.

What starts out as a familiar nursery rhyme soon changes! What happens is that the woman who goes to market continues to get unruly animals so that when she gets home, she has a new situation to deal with. The animals take the exhausted and cranky woman back to the store so that she can buy several vegetables to make a fine soup for lunch.

Book Extender: A lesson on compare/contrast is a natural for this text. Have students compare it with the original rhyme. Invite students to talk about why they think the animals in this tale were so unruly and why they had the woman buy and cook only vegetables in her soup.

Today I Feel Silly and Other Moods That Make My Day
Jamie Lee Curtis, Author
Laura Cornell, Illustrator
New York: HarperCollins. 1998. 0-06-024560-3.

The text and illustrations—along with the accompanying mood wheel that shows different facial expressions to accompany each mood—encourage children to explore their different moods. The children are also encouraged to identify how they are feeling and to have fun with the particular mood they are experiencing.

 Focus on Phonological Awareness (phoneme deletion): After reading through the book for enjoyment, focus on phonological awareness by having children tell you which sounds were deleted to create new words in this story.

1. What sound do I take away from *clear* to make *ear?*
2. What sound do I take away from *shout* to make *out?*
3. What sound do I take away from *hair* to make *air?*

Toddlerobics: Animal Fun
Zita Newcome, Author and Illustrator
Cambridge, MA: Candlewick. 1999. 0-7636-0803-3.

The children in this book are no different from many children: they like to pretend to be other creatures. In this book, the children like to move like different animals. Get ready for listeners of this story to do the same as they will want to join the fun!

Top Cat
Lois Ehlert, Author and Illustrator
San Diego: Harcourt. 1998. 0-15-201739-9.

Top Cat is the ruler of the house—at least until a new kitty arrives. Although reluctant to give up some of his territory, Top Cat finally concedes and shows Little Kitty how to perform many different "cat" activities. Using rhyme, this book is written in first person, enabling the listener or reader to imagine the behaviors of cats.

The Turning of the Year
Bill Martin Jr., Author
Greg Shed, Illustrator
San Diego: Harcourt. 1998. 0-15-201085-8.

While the text remains the same as when this book was first published in 1970, the illustrations breathe new life into it. The rhyming text describes each month in simple verse.

📖 *Book Extender:* Brainstorm a list of activities that children do in each month of the year. Or make a list of activities that children complete within a given month. This could be an ongoing activity, and completed month charts could be displayed in the room.

Twinkle, Twinkle: An Animal Lover's Mother Goose
Bobbi Fabian, Illustrator
New York: Dutton. 1996. 0-525-45906-5.

In this version of familiar Mother Goose rhymes, the words remain the same but the pictures change. Different animals, rather than people, are depicted for each rhyme. Photographs are used with paintings, making the rhymes take on a whole new look!

Uno, Dos, Tres; One, Two, Three
Pat Mora, Author
Barbara Lavalle, Illustrator
New York: Clarion. 1996. 0-395-67294-5.

Two girls go from store to store to buy birthday presents for their mother. Readers are provided with opportunities to read the numbers one through ten in Spanish and English. A pronunciation guide is provided at the end of the book.

Up the Ladder, Down the Slide
Betsy Everitt, Author and Illustrator
San Diego:

This book invites youngsters to experience a picnic in the park. Between saying "hello" and saying "so long," children experience many activities.

📖 *Book Extender:* Provide children with simple props as mentioned in the text, and encourage them to use the props as they perform or retell the story.

Wake Up/Sleep Tight
Ken Wilson-Max, Author and Illustrator
New York: Scholastic. 1998. 0-590-76779-8.

From morning till night, there are many activities for a young child to accomplish in a day. A clock with movable hands is part of the book, inviting the reader or listener to move the hands to the time indicated on the page.

Warthogs in the Kitchen: A Sloppy Counting Book
Pamela Duncan Edwards, Author
Henry Cole, Illustrator
New York: Hyperion. 1998. 0-7868-2351-8.

Come discover what happens when the warthogs decide to bake cupcakes! The story is told in simple, rhythmic text. Readers and listeners will chuckle as they experience this humorous book and at the same time learn about numbers zero through ten. The watercolor illustrations add to the humor by showing the warthogs in action. For those who want to make cupcakes of their own, cupcake recipes—for both humans and warthogs—are provided on the last page of the book.

Focus on Phonological Awareness (syllables): Invite children to clap for the word parts as you say these two-syllable words: *today, away; ready, teddy; tummy, yummy.*

Book Extender: Invite children to use the numbers zero through ten to create another book that explains how to create something.

What's Alice Up To?
Harley Jessup, Author and Illustrator
New York: Viking. 1997. 0-670-87396-9.

Alice has a curious dog, and as he watches her complete many activities, he begins to feel a little angry that she will not let him in on the secret of why she is doing what she is doing. All ends well, however, as the dog soon discovers that all of Alice's activities have to do with preparing a nice birthday surprise, for the dog, no less!

What Do You See When You Shut Your Eyes?
Cynthia Zarin, Author
Sarah Durham, Illustrator
Boston: Houghton Mifflin. 1998. 0-395-76507-2.

The children in this story explore their various senses as they shut one eye and take a look at what they see with the one that remains open. They then explore sounds in their environment as they listen and sing. They help us see that we can view the world in many different ways.

📖 *Book Extender:* Because the characters explore their senses, this book can be used as an introduction to the five senses. After reading it, have students view their worlds in a similar manner. For example, have them close their eyes and listen to all the sounds they hear. After a couple of minutes, have them open their eyes and state what they heard.

When It Starts to Snow
Phillis Gershator, Author
Martin Matje, Illustrator
New York: Holt. 1998. 0-8050-5404-9.

What do different animals do when it snows? Where do they go? The rhyming text used to create this book provides the answers to these questions for each animal. The colorful illustrations add to the text by providing a glimpse of each animal doing what it says as it snows.

 Focus on Phonological Awareness (phoneme matching): This book provides many words that contain the /ō/ sound. To help children discover this, provide them with pictures of objects mentioned in the book along with others that do not fit the category. Next, ask children to sort the pictures, placing those that have the /ō/ sound in one category and those that don't in a second category.

When the Wind Bears Go Dancing
Phoebe Stone, Author and Illustrator
New York: Little, Brown. 1997. 0-316-81701-5.

Come on a midnight adventure to discover what happens when the wind blows in the night. This is exactly what the young girl in this story does as she joins five woolly wind bears on their escapades one night. Fear not, however! She lands at home safe and snug in bed.

📖 *Book Extender:* The wind bears perform a wind dance as they romp through the night. Invite students to dance like they think the bears might dance as you read through the book a second time.

When Mama Comes Home Tonight
Eileen Spinelli, Author
Jane Dyer, Illustrator
New York: Simon & Schuster. 1998. 0-689-81065-2.

A child waits for what seems an eternity for her mother to come home from work. Once home, the child and mother complete rituals that celebrate their time together. The rhythmic text is comforting and shows how even the simplest of tasks can be memorable when performed with a person you love.

Where Are Mary's Pets?
Clive Scruton, Author and Illustrator
Cambridge, MA: Candlewick. 1999. 0-7636-0760-6.

Mary wants to play with her pets, but they seem to have disappeared. She goes in search of them and, one by one, finds each and every one of them. Rhyming text provides clues to each pet that is hiding behind a flap on each page.

🎺 *Focus on Phonological Awareness (phoneme manipulation):* Say one of the words from the text and ask students what they need to change to turn it into another word that rhymes with the one you say. For example, "What do I need to do to change *in* to *grin*?" (add /g/ /r/)

📖 *Book Extender:* This is an excellent book for helping children learn to piece together some clues to make inferences. Using a think-aloud, model for students which words can be used to help make an inference about the hidden animal. Then have children create their own riddles.

Where Did Josie Go?
Helen E. Buckley, Author
Jan Ormerod, Illustrator
New York: Lothrop. 1999. 0-688-16507-9.

All children have participated in hiding games, and they will enjoy this book as a result. Josie hides from her parents and they go in search of her. Of course, part of Josie is revealed in each picture, but the parents play along and pretend that they cannot see her. The game ends when Josie reveals her whole self in the hammock.

Where Does Joe Go?
Tracey Campbell Pearson, Author and Illustrator
New York: Farrar, Straus & Giroux. 1999. 0-374-38319-7.

Joe runs the local snack bar at the beach and closes it during the off-seasons. This leads the townspeople to wonder where he goes when his snack bar is closed. They let their imaginations run wild as they speculate about all the places he might go. Will he tell when he returns? Absolutely not, but a look at the last page provides a clue.

Wherever Bears Be
Sue Ann Alderson, Author
Arden Johnson, Illustrator
Berkeley, CA: Tricycle. 1999. 1-883672-77-5.

Two young girls go berry picking only to discover that bears like berries, too. Fortunately, all of the bears the girls encounter are friendly. In fact, they are so friendly that they hide as they watch the girls, making the girls believe that there are no bears in the mountains. Little do they know!

Window Music
Anastasia Suen, Author
Wade Zahares, Illustrator
New York: Viking. 1998. 0-670-87287-3.

Climb aboard and vicariously experience riding a train by listening to or reading this book. From the clickety-clack sounds made by the train on the track to the station—the final destination—readers experience the many sights and sounds of a train ride.

📖 *Book Extender:* This book is a natural for encouraging students to tell about train rides they may have taken—where they boarded, where they went, and what they saw along the way. The book can also be used as a catalyst for inviting students to tell about other modes of transportation they have used when vacationing.

Winter Lullaby
Barbara Seuling, Author
Greg Newbold, Illustrator
San Diego: Browndeer/Harcourt. 1998. 0-15-201403-9.

Simple, rhythmic text is used to explain how different animals survive during winter. From bats that sleep in caverns to fish that swim deeper where water is warmer, many different animals are depicted. The vivid illustrations show both the external world and the inner worlds where the animals survive.

📖 *Book Extender:* Use this book to help children understand the difference between a question and a statement. The question/answer format lends itself well to this. After pointing this out, pair students. Have one ask a question and another state a complete response to the question.

Winter Visitors
Elizabeth Lee O'Donnell, Author
Carol Schwartz, Illustrator
New York: Morrow. 1997. 0-688-13063-1.

Where do animals go when it snows? In this rhyming text, they go straight into a house, making themselves welcome to the many amenities they find. Fortunately, they can be persuaded to return to the woods—all except Shopie, the skunk, that is!

The Wizard
Bill Martin Jr., Author
Alex Schaefer, Illustrator
San Diego: Voyager/Harcourt. 1997. 0-15-201568-X.

This is the story of a wizard who performs many actions to create a potion. In all of the activity, however, the pot gets knocked over, causing the potion to spill and eventually the wizard to disappear. The story is told in very simple sentences—containing one to four words.

 Focus on Phonological Awareness (phoneme substitution): Select rhyming words from the text and use them to help students become wizards with phoneme substitution. You will need a prop that can function as a wizard's magic wand. Tell students that you need a volunteer to be the wizard, zapping a sound at the beginning of a word and replacing it with another sound to create a new word. Provide statements such as, "Zap the /s/ in *sing* and add a letter to make a word that names a part of a bird." (*wing*) Other sample words from the text that can be used are: *flip, flop; dip, dop; growl, prowl, owl; pong, dong; stumble, tumble*.

Worksong
Gary Paulsen, Author
Ruth Wright Paulsen, Illustrator
San Diego: Harcourt. 1997. 0-15-200980-9.

The rhythmic text and colorful, detailed illustrations show people doing all kinds of work. This text shows children the many different kinds of jobs that contribute to a functional society.

📖 *Book Extender*: Encourage children to talk about the kind of job they would like to have when they grow up.

Yum, Yum, All Done
Jerry Smath, Author and Illustrator
New York: Grosset and Dunlap. 1998. 0-448-41745-6.

Through die-cut pages, children discover how baby animals finish their dinners. Told in simple, rhyming text, this book will engage youngsters as they flip the pages to discover what's hidden behind each page.

Focus on Phonological Awareness (phoneme addition): Some of the rhyming words used in this text are created by deleting the initial sound. During a second reading, point out these words and ask students to tell you the sound that was deleted. You might say something like this: "Say *able*. Now say it with /t/at the beginning. What's the word?" (*table*)

3

Alliterative Texts

Peter Piper picked a . . . You finish it! Perhaps as fun and helpful as rhyme in developing a sense for the sounds in our language, alliteration is a series of two or more words that begin with the same sound. Alliteration helps children develop a sense of wordness because the same beginning sound serves as a boundary in the speech stream, signaling when a new word begins. And attention to beginning sounds also helps children understand that sounds in words come in a specific order; manipulating the sounds alters the word.

This section includes the most recently published children's literature in which the authors use alliteration to convey their ideas to the reader or listener. As with other chapters in this book, many of these titles are followed by activities that either help students better understand an aspect of their spoken language or extend the book in some way.

A Is for Amos
Deborah Chandra, Author
Keiko Narahashi, Illustrator
New York: Farrar, Straus & Giroux. 1999. 0-374-30001-1.

What do you get when you use a little imagination while sitting on a rocking horse? All sorts of adventures as you pretend that the rocking horse is a live animal. Climb on Amos and take an imaginary ride and gallop through objects that are associated with every letter of the alphabet.

A Pair of Protoceratops
Bernard Most, Author and Illustrator
San Diego: Harcourt. 1998. 0-15-302443-8.

Join in the fun by playing with a pair of protoceratops as they complete many different activities, such as preparing for preschool!

 Focus on Phonological Awareness (alliteration): Have students repeat words that begin with the sound of /p/. Or create a list of words that begin with /p/.

A Trio of Triceratops
Bernard Most, Author and Illustrator
San Diego: Harcourt. 1998. 0-15-201448-9.

This books shows a trio of triceratops having a lot of fun as they complete activities that begin with the /t/ sound. From touching their toes to trying on towels, youngsters will enjoy seeing the many things the trio accomplishes.

ABC Discovery!
Izhar Cohen, Author and Illustrator
New York: Dial/Penguin. 1997. 0-8037-2321-0.

Discover the many objects and actions that are associated with each letter of the alphabet as shown in this book. Each two-page spread shows a list of words beginning with the letter on the left and a picture showing many of the words being used. Cohen also invites readers to look again at the book to try to solve the many discovery puzzles she poses at the end of the book. Finding objects throughout the book that begin with a given letter is just one of the many discovery puzzles she lists.

 Focus on Phonological Awareness (alliteration): Invite students to say a sentence about the picture shown on the right-hand side. The trick? Trying to start each word in the sentence with the sound associated with the letter.

The Absolutely Awful Alphabet
Mordicai Gerstein, Author and Illustrator
San Diego: Harcourt. 1999. 0-15-201494-2.

In this book, the alphabet is anything but nice. Each letter takes on a personality of its own and through alliterative verse, the listener or reader discovers both the name of the creature and what that creature wants to do to another creature. Of course, each creature is designed to be the shape of the letter it represents. From A, the awfully arrogant amphibian, to Z, a zigzaggin zoological zany, children will make many surprising discoveries.

 Focus on Phonological Awareness (sounds): Have children say the sound they hear at the beginning of the words given for any letter of the alphabet.

📖 *Book Extender:* Have children create their own creature for a given letter of the alphabet and give it a name that begins with the sound associated with the letter. As a class or individually, have students create an alliterative verse for their creature, but have the creature do good deeds rather than bad ones like those mentioned in the text.

The Accidental Zucchini: An Unexpected Alphabet
Max Grover, Author and Illustrator
San Diego: Voyager/Harcourt. 1997. 0-15-201545-0.

In this award-winning book, each letter of the alphabet is represented by a combination of objects, all of which begin with the same letter. The illustrations depict each two-word description. From apple autos to the zigzag zoo, children will see many imaginative objects.

 Focus on Phonological Awareness: Have children create their own object for a letter of the alphabet and a two-word label for it, each word beginning with the same sound.

Alice and Aldo
Alison Lester, Author and Illustrator
Boston: Houghton Mifflin. 1998. 0-395-87092.

A busy day in the life of Alice and Aldo, her toy donkey, is revealed in this delightful text. From A to Z, from sunrise to sunset, Alice and Aldo keep themselves busy and at the same time have a lot of fun. Many pictures are provided for each letter of the alphabet, and all are labeled.

 Focus on Phonological Awareness (sound isolation): Invite children to say the names of the pictures shown on each page and to determine how all are alike. You might say something such as this: "Now that you've listened to me read the story, let's go back and take another look at the pictures. I'll name each one and you tell me the sound you hear at the beginning of each."

Alison's Zinnia
Anita Lobel, Author and Illustrator
New York: Greenwillow. 1990. 0-688-08865-1.

Alison and others whose names begin with a different letter of the alphabet discover many different types of flowers that begin with the same sound as their name. This is why Alison acquires an Amarylis for Beryl and so on. Each verse is accompanied by a full-page illustration of the named flower.

Animal Parade
Jakki Wood, Author and Illustrator
New York: Scholastic. 1994. 0-590-48218-1.

The animals go on parade in this text that feels a lot like alliteration. Animal names are listed for each letter of the alphabet on the bottom of the page. The illustrations show all listed animals.

Away from Home
Anita Lobel, Author and Illustrator
New York: Greenwillow. 1994. 0-688-10354-5.

Using alliterative text, Lobel takes readers on a journey around the world. Using boys' names for each letter of the alphabet, she has each visit a place that begins with the same sound (letter). Thus, "Adam arrived in Amsterdam and Zachary zigzagged in Zaandam." A list of all of the places where the boys travel is provided in the back of the book.

Focus on Phonological Awareness (phoneme matching): Using the pattern established in the book, have each student create a place to travel using the first sound in their names. For example, "Brad bounced to the bakery." Or "Holly hopped home."

The Awful Aardvarks Go to School
Reeve Lindbergh, Author
Tracey Campbell Pearson, Illustrator
New York: Viking. 1997. 0-670-85920-6.

This is a story about some mischievous aardvarks during a visit to school. Their acts of destruction begin with *a* and proceed to *z* and provide several alliterative rhymes that tell of the chaos created by these critters in a class that is trying to be attentive.

Elfabet: An ABC of Elves
Jane Yolen, Author
Lauren Mills, Illustrator
New York: Little, Brown. 1990. 0-316-96888-9.

This book is a collection of elves from A to Z, one for each letter of the alphabet. Each elf takes on a different personality and is surrounded by objects that begin with the same letter.

 Focus on Phonological Awareness: Invite children to locate the objects in the picture that begin with the sound of the letter being shown.

Emma's Elephant and Other Favorite Animal Friends
David Ellwand, Author and Photographer
New York: Dutton. 1997. 0-525-45792-5.

Full-page photographs show different children with different animals that begin with the letter of the child's name, creating a simple alliterative verse such as "Simon's slithery snake."

📖 *Book Extender:* As in the book, have children choose an object that begins with the same sound as their name. Take a picture of each child holding the object and write a verse underneath it. Gather the children together and provide time for each child to share. When they finish, compile all pictures in a class book for the classroom library collection.

Fast Freddie Frog and Other Tongue-Twister Rhymes
Ennis Rees, Author
John O'Brien, Illustrator
Honesdale, PA: Boyds Mills. 1993. 1-56397-038-4.

This is a collection of alliterative verses that are quite a challenge to say. Have fun trying to say these humorous rhymes—and do try to keep your tongue from getting all twisted.

Four Famished Foxes and Fosdyke
Pamela Duncan Edwards, Author
Henry Cole, Illustrator
New York: HarperTrophy. 1997. 0-06-443480-X.

This is the story of five foxes whose names begin with /f/ and their attempts to gather food for themselves. One day their mother decides that they can fend for themselves and she heads off to Florida. While she's away, the four foxes go hunting for food in the barnyard while their vegetarian brother prepares a vegetarian feast in which all partake after their unsuccessful attempts to gather food in the barnyard. At least sixty words beginning with /f/ are used to create this alliterative, tongue-twister text.

 Focus on Phonological Awareness: On a second read of the text, have children clap every time they hear a word beginning with /f/.

Goblins in Green
Nicholas Heller, Author
Jos. A. Smith, Illustrator
New York: Greenwillow. 1995. 0-688-12802-5.

Two children take a peek through a trap door and discover green goblins getting dressed in clothes. From A to Z, the goblins dress themselves in clothing that corresponds to the first letter in their names. So, while Annabelle wears an amber blouse, Yolanda yodels in her yellow zoot suit. Each short alliterative verse also includes a word that begins with the next letter of the alphabet.

Miss Spider's ABC
David Kirk, Author and Illustrator
New York: Scholastic. 1998. 0-590-28279-4.

Miss Spider's friends create a surprise birthday party for her in this alliterative text. Each page focuses on a letter by featuring an invited guest whose name begins with a particular letter of the alphabet and what the guest is doing to prepare for the surprise—all of the words beginning with the given letter.

 Focus on Phonological Awareness (phoneme matching): Have children create their own alphabet birthday feast by having them bring something to the party that begins with the same letter of the alphabet as their name.

Pignic
Anne Miranda, Author
Rosekrans Hoffman, Illustrator
Honesdale, PA: Boyds Mills. 1996. 1-56397-558-0.

If humans enjoy picnics, what do pigs enjoy? You guessed it: pignics! This is the story of one such pignic, the annual family pignic. Each family member brings something that begins with the same sound as his or her name.

 Focus on Phonological Awareness (phoneme matching): Take children on an imaginary or real picnic, asking them to bring something that begins with the sound that begins their name.

Some Smug Slug
Pamela Duncan Edwards, Author
Henry Cole, Illustrator
New York: HarperTrophy. 1996. 0-06-443502-4.

In this alliterative, tongue-twisting adventure, a slug makes his way to the summit in spite of the warnings provided by the animals he passes on his journey. His success is short-lived, as a toad gobbles him up.

📖 *Book Extender:* This book lends itself well to sequencing and dramatization. Invite students to take on the roles of the different animals and have them act out the story by calling out, in order, their warning as stated in the book. An added feature could be a class-created mural representing different places through which the slug slinks. With the mural completed, children representing the different animals could stand or sit in place and say their part as the slug slinks past them.

The Wacky Wedding: A Book of Alphabet Antics
Pamela Duncan Edwards, Author
Henry Cole, Illustrator
New York: Hyperion. 1999. 0-7868-2248-1.

Usually, weddings are performed with few problems. Not so for the unfortunate ants who decide to get married in this story! One mishap leads to the next. In fact, there is one for each letter of the alphabet. All ends well, however. Children will not only enjoy the alliterative text but will also enjoy the challenge of finding the letters hidden in the pictures.

Watch William Walk
Ann Jonas, Author and Illustrator
New York: Greenwillow. 1997. 0-688-14172-2.

William and Wilma take a walk with their dog and duck, Wally and Wanda. In this alliterative text—all words begin with /w/—they all experience many activities along the way.

4

Repetitive Texts

When thinking about appropriate books to nurture phonological awareness, you may think it odd to include a chapter that provides titles that use repetitive text. And your thinking may be right on if it is centered on best ways to help children develop an ear for the sounds of their language and on the fact that words are made up of individual sounds that have been grouped together in a given order (i.e., *phonemic awareness*). The children's literature described in the other chapters in this book will best help accomplish this awareness.

Recall, though, that there are three stages of *phonological awareness* and that the first two stages to develop are the understanding that words are sound units that can be strung together in the speech stream to communicate with others and that these words are made up of word parts (i.e., syllables). As mentioned earlier (see Chapter 1), children's literature is one of the best ways to foster *all three* of these stages.

Including authentic children's literature that employs repetition is necessary to nurture these other aspects of phonological awareness. Through repetition, children see the same symbols over and over again and gradually come to understand that these symbols (i.e., letters) are grouped together to form words (Snow et al. 1998). That is, they develop a concept of *wordness*. They also begin to see that some words are longer than others and that longer words have more parts (i.e., syllables). And, of course, the repetition makes the books excellent choices for shared reading because they provide enough support to enable even the most novice of readers to join in the reading and to discover how written language is used to create meaningful, engaging stories. Doing so provides children with an opportunity to produce the words themselves. Thus, they get a feel for how different words feel when they are spoken and see that spoken language is connected with print.

Finally, most repetitive texts employ a pattern sentence. Consider DeMunn's *The Earth Is Good: A Chant in Praise of Nature*, described later in this chapter. The sentence pattern used to create this text is "The _____ is good." Text such as this invites further language play by providing a pattern that students can use to create their own sentences; they innovate on the text, and this experience furthers their understanding and finesse with manipulating language. And, as some of the phonological awareness activities in this chapter show, repetitive texts can also be used to help children develop phonemic awareness!

Clearly, then, using repetitive text is important. Fortunately, there are many superb representative titles. This chapter lists many of those most recently published.

Baby Bird
Joyce Dunbar, Author
Russell Ayto, Illustrator
Cambridge, MA: Candlewick. 1998. 0-7636-0322-8.

The baby bird in this text wants to accomplish one thing—flying! And persist he does, meeting different animals along the way. At long last he meets with success, flying over all those he previously encountered.

Book Extender: Use this book as a catalyst for a discussion about different activities children have tried and how sticking with an activity enabled them to succeed. Encourage children to share their experiences.

Big and Little
Margaret Miller, Author and Photographer
New York: Greenwillow. 1998. 0-688-14748-8.

In simple verse, Miller helps children better understand the opposites big and little. Photographs show children completing different activities or in different sizes and are accompanied by the text "Big _____, Little _____." While most verses lack rhyming, they carry a distinct rhythm, giving the feel of a jump rope jingle.

Focus on Phonological Awareness: Using words from the various verses, ask students to state which one is not like the other two. Here are some sample sets:

1. foot, *grow*, foot
2. hand, hand, *tight*
3. *go*, dog, dog
4. hat, hat, *up*
5. truck, *ride*, truck
6. *me*, girl, girl
7. ball, ball, *down*
8. *house*, block, block

☐ *Book Extender:* Invite students to create their own "Big and Little" opposites books. These could include photographs of themselves doing different activities at different times in their lives—and would serve as an excellent way to involve parents.

The Big Wide-Mouthed Frog
Ana Martin Larranaga, Author and Illustrator
Cambridge, MA: Candlewick. 1999. 0-7636-0807-6.

Much repetition drives home the point that the frog in this story eats flies; he tells all the animals he meets! But what about the other animals? What do they eat? Big Wide-Mouthed Frog discovers.

☐ *Book Extender:* Invite students to investigate what other animals eat. A good place to begin might be to have them talk about their pets and what they feed them.

Cat's Colors
Jane Cabrera, Author and Illustrator
New York: Dial. 1997. 0-8037-2090-4.

What is the cat's favorite color? This is the recurring question that takes readers through basic colors and objects that are associated with them. Of course, orange has to be the favorite color because that's the color of Cat's mother!

☐ *Book Extender:* A logical follow-up to this story is to invite students to name their favorite colors and then to either draw or locate pictures of objects that show their favorite color. Children can also label each object. These could be assembled in a book for the classroom library entitled "Our Favorite Colors."

Cherry Pies and Lullabies
Lynn Reiser, Author and Illustrator
New York: Greenwillow. 1998. 0-688-13391-6.

Family traditions are explored in this simple repetitive text as four generations of mothers and daughters participate in the same activities. From making cherry pies to singing lullabies, listeners and readers are invited to experience timeless activities that also express love for one another. A lullaby with accompanying music is included.

 Focus on Phonological Awareness (phoneme matching): Because this book focuses on same/different, use it as a catalyst for playing "same/different" with students. Explain how the game is played by saying something such as, "I will say two words. If they sound the same, you say 'same'; if they are not exactly alike, if they sound different, say, 'different.'" Sample word pairs from the book include the following:

1. pie, for
2. baked, baked
3. bear, bear
4. time, the

📖 *Book Extender:* Ask children to think of activities they do that are like those completed in the book. Children can also be invited to ask their parents which activities have been passed down through the generations. Perhaps a form like the one shown below could be used as a structure when interviewing parents.

Name of activity:_____
Grandmother/father for _____
Mother/father for_____
(Child's name) for_____

Chili-Chili-Chin-Chin
Belle Yang, Author and Illustrator
San Diego: Silver Whistle/Harcourt. 1999. 0-15-202006-3.

This is the story of friendship between a young boy and his donkey. As seen through the donkey's eyes, friendship is based on mutual respect and concern for one another.

Daddy Will Be There
Lois Grambling, Author
Walter Gaffney-Kessell, Illustrator
New York: Greenwillow. 1998. 0-688-14983-9.

The main message contained in this book is that no matter what happens, Daddy will be there to help solve the problem. This is a comforting realization to the little girl in this text as she goes about completing several activities to expand her horizons with confidence.

 Focus on Phonological Awareness (syllables): Multisyllabic words are used to create this text. Therefore, play "1, 2, 3." Here's how: Invite children to clap the word parts they hear after you say a word and then hold up the number of fingers representing the number of parts they clapped. Sample words from the book include the following:

1. play (1)	2. alone (2)	3. picture (2)	4. kitchen (2)
5. Daddy (2)	6. my (1)	7. alligator (3)	8. blueberry (3)

📖 *Book Extender:* The girl in this text completes several different activities. A logical extension is to invite students to tell about some of the activities they complete on their own.

The Earth Is Good: A Chant in Praise of Nature
Michael DeMunn, Author
Jim McMullan, Illustrator
New York: Scholastic. 1999. 0-590-35010-2.

Here's a chant that teaches children to appreciate the many gifts of the earth. But perhaps most important, the chant helps children to discover that they are one of the earth's greatest gifts.

📖 *Book Extender:* The sentence pattern used in this text is "The _____ is good." Invite children to use this sentence, either orally or in writing, filling in something that they think is good.

The Football That Won . . .
Michael Sampson, Author
Ted Rand, Illustrator
New York: Holt. 1996. 0-8050-3504-4.

Some people think that it's the football team that wins a football game. This book provides the rest of the story by telling it from the football's perspective. Yes, indeed, winning probably does have a lot to do with the football and its desire to win the game!

Go Tell It to the Toucan
Colin West, Author and Illustrator
Cambridge, MA: Candlewick. 1990. 1-56402-600-0.

Today is Elephant's birthday and he knows just who to tell to spread the word: Toucan. One by one, Toucan informs all the other jungle animals, and they all join together for a birthday jamboree!

Hello, Fox
Eric Carle, Author and Illustrator
New York: Simon & Schuster. 1998. 0-689-81775-4.

In this fun, engaging book, youngsters are invited to see the colors of the various animals that Mother Frog has invited to Little Frog's birthday party. Children also learn something about colors along the way because all the illustrations are designed to show complimentary colors on the color wheel.

📖 *Book Extender:* Because the animals come to the party in a specific order, this book lends itself well to sequencing story events. Assign students different roles and invite them to come to the party in the same order as the characters did in the text.

I Love You, Little One
Nancy Tafuri, Author and Illustrator
New York: Scholastic. 1998. 0-590-92159-2.

Six different animals ask their mothers for assurance of their love. In their responses, the mothers share the many different ways that they love their children forever and always.

🎺 *Focus on Phonological Awareness (syllables):* Many multisyllabic words are used to create this text. Have students hold up one, two, or three fingers to show how many parts they hear. Sample words include the following:

1. woods (1)   2. riverbank (3)   3. singing (2)   4. always (2)
5. duck (1)   6. mossy (2)   7. burrow (2)   8. shelter (2)

📖 *Book Extender:* While this book can be used at any time of the year, it could be especially effective around Valentine's Day since the holiday focuses on love and friendship. Invite children to talk about how they know they are loved by others and how they let others know that they love them.

I See the Moon and the Moon Sees Me
Jonathan London, Author
Peter Fiore, Illustrator
New York: Viking. 1996. 0-670-85918-4.

In the adaptation of this familiar nursery rhyme, a young boy sees several different objects throughout the day. He talks to each as he sees them. Many aspects of nature are explored as a result.

📖 *Book Extender:* Take children on a nature walk and have them identify one object they see. Back in the classroom, use the same sentence pattern as used in the text to have them tell what they saw. If these are also written and illustrated, assemble them into a book for the classroom library entitled "What We See."

I Spy Two Eyes: Numbers in Art
Lucy Micklethwait, Author and Compiler
New York: Mulberry. 1998. 0-688-16158-8.

Famous paintings are used to help children understand numbers through twenty. The repetitive line "I Spy" invites children to chime right in as they explore the famous paintings to discover the objects mentioned.

📖 *Book Extender:* Provide time for children to make their own hidden pictures. Place numbers in a bag (making sure to have enough for each child). Have children draw a number out of the bag and draw a picture in which they hide an object the number of times shown on their card.

Kate's Castle
Julie Lawson, Author
Frances Tyrrell, Illustrator
Toronto, Canada: Stoddart. 1997. 0-7737-5899-2.

Based on the same pattern as *This Is the House That Jack Built*, this is the story of a castle that Kate builds. She collects different objects for her castle, helping those who read or listen to this book learn about sea creatures.

Little Clam
Lynn Reiser, Author and Illustrator
New York: Greenwillow. 1998. 0-688-15908-7.

Sometimes we have to hear something more than once to believe it. Such is the case in this book. Little Clam is warned several times that he needs to dig in the sand to escape the other animals who would just as soon have him for dinner. He digs in and just in the nick of time! A clam game that can be played by parent and child is provided in the back of the text.

 Focus on Phonological Awareness (syllables): Show students how to place their hands together so that they can pretend to be clams. Next, tell them that you will say a word. If it has two parts, like a clam's shell, they are to open their hands (clam). Sample words from the text include the following:

1. clam (1)	2. siphons (2)	3. tide (1)	4. awake (2)
5. already (3)	6. listening (3)	7. scallop (2)	8. hungry (2)

Mama Cat Has Three Kittens
Denise Fleming, Author and Illustrator
New York: Holt. 1998. 0-8050-5745-5.

Two of the three kittens in this book do exactly as their mother does. However, one kitten does nothing but nap until all the others are napping. He then wakes up and, after playing for a short while, pounces on his mother to nap once again. A hidden surprise is that on every page another animal appears somewhere in the picture.

Me and You: A Mother-Daughter Album
Lisa Thiesing, Author and Illustrator
New York: Hyperion. 1998. 0-7868-2338-0.

Through pictures, a mother shows her daughter that she was similar to her in many ways when she was a baby. Beginning with baby pictures and continuing through good and bad behaviors, readers and listeners will share in the many likenesses and memories.

🎺 *Focus on Phonological Awareness (word):* Reread some of the sentences and have children count the number of words they hear as you read.

📖 *Book Extender:* This book could be used as part of a unit on relationships. Have children create a similar book with their parents. (Boys could create a book with their fathers.)

Moo Moo, Brown Cow
Jakki Wood, Author
Rog Bonner, Illustrator
San Diego: Gulliver/Harcourt. 1992. 0-15-200533-1.

How many chicks does the hen have? How many piglets does the pig have? Answers to these questions and others are provided in this book as several different animals are presented.

One Moose, Twenty Mice
Clare Beaton, Author and Illustrator
New York: Barefoot. 1999. 1-902283-37-6.

The big, repeating question in this book is "Where's the cat?" After counting several different animals, we finally get an answer to the question: the cat is with the twenty mice!

Say Something
Mary Stolz, Author
Alexander Koshkin, Illustrator
New York: HarperCollins. 1993. 0-06-021158-X.

A father and his son go on a fishing trip and play "say something." The father tells the boy about whatever is asked for. In this way, the young boy learns a lot about nature.

Sleep, Little One, Sleep
Marion Dane Bauer, Author
JoEllen McAllister Stammen, Illustrator
New York: Simon & Schuster. 1999. 0-689-82250-2.

A father puts his child to bed by telling how actions of various animals help to enable a sound sleep. With captivating illustrations to accompany each verse, the story is told as a lullaby, and the last phrase of each verse is repeated. From the spider that spins a web to cradle the whale that encourages a deep, deep sleep, all children are sure to take comfort in discovering how animals help to create a restful sleep.

Things That Are Most in the World
Judi Barrett, Author
John Nickle, Illustrator
New York: Atheneum. 1998. 0-689-81333-3.

Discover some of the silliest, heaviest, and smelliest things in the world! This book shows several objects representing each superlative in imaginative ways. Barrett encourages students to write and draw their own thing that's most in their world by providing a page in the back of the book. Permission is granted to photocopy.

 Focus on Phonological Awareness (sound deletion): To help students better understand word parts, play take-away. Tell students to provide the word to complete statements such as those that follow.

1. Take *-est* away from *wiggliest* and it will leave you with (*wiggly*).
2. Take *-est* away from *silliest* and it will leave you with (*silly*).
3. Take *-est* away from *quietest* and it will leave you with (*quiet*).
4. Take *-est* away from *prickliest* and it will leave you with (*prickly*).
5. Take *-est* away from *hottest* and it will leave you with (*hot*).

📖 *Book Extender:* Copy the last page of the book for each student and permit them to use their imagination to construct their "most" in the world. Once finished, gather students and have them share their "mosts." Finally, assemble all of their papers into a class book entitled something like "Our Mosts in the World."

This Is the Bread I Baked for End
Crescent Dragonwagon, Author
Isadore Sletzer, Illustrator
New York: Aladdin. 1999. 0-689-82353-3.

Using the story pattern used to create *This Is the House that Jack Built*, this text tells the story of a feast that Glenda prepares for End. However, several guests arrive to share the feast and in the cleanup!

This Train
Paul Collicutt, Author and Illustrator
New York: Farrar, Straus & Giroux. 1999. 0-374-37493-7.

With the simple sentence pattern "This train is _____," this book shows many different kinds of trains. It also shows where they travel and what they carry—rain, snow, or sunshine!

Focus on Phonological Awareness (word): As you reread the book, have children count the number of words in given sentences.

Book Extender: You might want to use the basic sentence structure and invite children to tell about another mode of transportation. For example, the sentence could be changed to "The car is _____."

Tick-Tock
Lena Anderson, Author and Illustrator
New York: Farrar, Straus & Giroux. 1998. 91-29-64074-1.

Here's a book that teaches telling time along with reading. All of the activities that Hedgehog, Duck, Elephant, and Pig complete with Will are associated with specific times of the day. Beginning with one o'clock and going to the park, and ending with midnight, when Will finally gets to sleep, readers and listeners experience many happenings.

Focus on Phonological Awareness (word): The sentences that make up this text are perfect for helping students further understand that sentences are composed of words. Say each sentence and have students count the number of words. Cross-check with the text after they give their responses.

Tortillas and Lullabies/Tortillas y Cancioncitas
Lynn Reiser, Author
Corazones Valientes, Illustrator
New York: Greenwillow. 1998. 0-68814628-7.

A young girl tells about family customs by explaining activities that her great-grandmother and grandmother did for their daughters—activities that she does for her doll. The simple repetitive text is written in both Spanish and English.

We Have a Baby
Cathryn Falwell, Author and Illustrator
New York: Clarion. 1993. 0-395-73970-5.

What does a baby need to feel loved? How do you care for a baby? In simple phrases, each beginning with "a baby to . . .," the text provides answers to these questions.

What the Sun Sees/What the Moon Sees
Nancy Tafuri, Author and Illustrator
New York: Greenwillow. 1997. 0-688-14493-4.

This book contrasts objects that are seen during the day with those seen at night. In one-line, repetitive sentences, the book starts with what the sun sees. A flip of the book starts the finished story all over again, this time showing what the moon sees in the night.

When I Am a Sister
Robin Ballard, Author and Illustrator
New York: Greenwillow. 1998. 0-688-15397-6.

A young child is told by her parents how the new baby will change their lives. Through their discussion, the parents reassure Kate that their love for her will not change. In fact, Kate is left with knowing that a few things will change and that change can be for the better. After all, she gets to be a big sister!

📖 *Book Extender:* Encourage students to tell about their role as big brother or big sister. What do they do to set a good example? How do they help their younger sibling(s)?

Who Hops?
Katie Davis, Author and Illustrator
San Diego: Harcourt. 1998. 0-15-201839-5.

This book helps children understand the different actions that animals perform. Some hop, whereas others swim. Told in simple, repetitive text, the book is divided into different sections (chapters) to classify animals according to how they move.

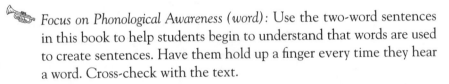 *Focus on Phonological Awareness (word):* Use the two-word sentences in this book to help students begin to understand that words are used to create sentences. Have them hold up a finger every time they hear a word. Cross-check with the text.

📖 *Book Extender:* Encourage children to discover other animals that hop or swim or do any other action mentioned in the book. These suggestions could be illustrated and compiled into a class book entitled "Who Hops? volume 2."

After reading the book, put the animal names on different cards. Then list the actions on other cards. Display the actions in the pocket holder and pass out one animal card to each student. In turn, have students place their cards under the correct action. Cross-check with the text.

Whose Ears?
Jeannette Rowe, Author and Illustrator
New York: Little, Brown. 1999. 0-316-75932-5.

Flip the many different flaps in this book to discover the answer to this re-curring question. Focusing first on their ears, the reader discovers many different animals. *Note:* Two additional books that follow this pattern (written by the same author and published by the same company) are *Whose Feet?* and *Whose Nose?*

Whose Hat?
Margaret Miller, Author and Photographer
New York: Mulberry. 1997. 0-688-15279-1.

Many hats are worn by people who complete many different types of jobs. This book invites readers to guess who wears the various kinds of hats fea-tured throughout the simple, repetitive text.

Will You Take Care of Me?
Margaret Park Bridges, Author
Melissa Sweet, Illustrator
New York: Morrow. 1998. 0-688-15194-9.

The basic message conveyed in this text is that no matter what, a parent's love remains constant. This message reassures Kangaroo, who may seek change yet still want his mother's love.

📖 *Book Extender:* Children could also be asked to play the "what-if" game. They think of a question beginning with "What if" and their parents could respond similar to the way the mother kangaroo does in the text.

Willy the Dreamer
Anthony Browne, Author and Illustrator
Cambridge, MA: Candlewick. 1998. 0-7636-0378-3.

Like many children, Willy dreams of becoming many different things. But what will he be? The question is left unanswered, but the book provides many possibilities through Willy's dreams.

🎺 *Focus on Phonological Awareness (word):* Because the sentences are car-ried over to two pages, this book could be an excellent source for helping students to understand that words, not pages, make sentences. Have them count the words as you read. You might then count the words as they watch to check their responses.

📖 *Book Extender:* While this book could be used throughout the year, using it to celebrate Martin Luther King Day seems appropriate. After reading this book and having children talk about and create their own dreams on paper, you could read or tell them about Martin Luther King's dream.

5

Poetry Texts:
Single-Poem Picture Books
and Collections

Since the beginning of time, it seems, poetry has been used to help children become better readers and more sensitive, enlightened members of society. As I was preparing this chapter, for example, I came across a volume published in 1903 that was used in school for recitation lessons. Many of the poems included were designed to teach children specific values as well. I couldn't help but wonder if the child who had once owned the book and whose name, etched in pen, was still visible on the title page, enjoyed the poems in the volume as much as I do now.

As in the past, poetry is used for a variety of reasons (Glazer and Lamme 1990). In this book, I suggest that poetry be used as a vehicle for helping children better understand the sound structure of their language. As they listen to poems, they develop a sense of how sounds are strung together to form words that convey intended meanings and images.

Numerous single-poem picture books, books that illustrate one poem, and collections of poems have been published recently. These are described in this chapter in two separate sections. Single-poem picture books are listed first, followed by poetry books that offer collections based on a common theme. As with other chapters in this book, many of the titles are accompanied by either phonological awareness activities, book-extension activities, or both.

Single-Poem Picture Books

Delicious Hullaboo/Pachanga Deliciosa
Pat Mora, Author
Francisco Mora, Illustrator
Houston: Piñata Books. 1998. 1-55885-246-8.

Beneath the desert moon, several creatures enjoy the company of one another as they share a delicious feast and listen to music provided by a mariachi band. Each verse is written in English and Spanish.

📖 *Book Extender:* Invite students to tell about the kinds of foods they eat and the activities they do when they are having a celebration with family and friends.

Earthsong
Sally Rogers, Author
Melissa Mathis, Illustrator
New York: Dutton. 1998. 0-525-45873-5.

Any person who has ever heard "Over in the Meadow" will soon recognize this poem. Using the same rhythmic, rhyming pattern, with dialogues between parents and their offspring, Rogers introduces youngsters to eleven animals from around the world. The book closes with notes related to each animal mentioned in the text.

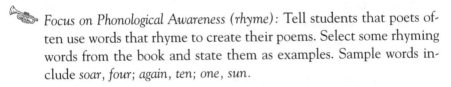 *Focus on Phonological Awareness (rhyme):* Tell students that poets often use words that rhyme to create their poems. Select some rhyming words from the book and state them as examples. Sample words include *soar, four; again, ten; one, sun.*

📖 *Book Extender:* Shared reading is a natural with this text. The teacher can take on the role of the parent and students can chime in when the child animal is speaking.

The Itsy Bitsy Spider
Illustrated by Lorianne Siomades
Honesdale, PA: Boyds Mills. 1999. 1-56397-727-3.

Vivid illustrations make this favorite rhyme an inviting read. Words are provided in large type and are juxtaposed with supportive illustrations that enable novice readers to read the text independently.

My Shadow
Robert Louis Stevenson, Author
Penny Dale, Illustrator
San Diego: Harcourt. 1999. 0-7636-0923-4.

With new illustrations, Dale breathes new life into this timeless piece that was created many years ago. It tells of a child discovering his shadow — something that every youngster enjoys discovering.

Focus on Phonological Awareness (phoneme matching): State a given sound and tell students that they are to tell you which word in the pair you state begins with the same sound.

Book Extender: Take children out to the playground on a sunny day and ask them questions such as these to help them learn more about their shadows: Do you have a shadow? Why? Is your shadow in front of you or in back of you? Does your shadow change size when you move? Does every person have a shadow?

The Owl and the Pussy-Cat
Edward Lear, Author
Ian Beck, Illustrator
New York: Atheneum. 1996. 0-689-81032-6.

New illustrations bring this favorite rhyme to life once again. Come discover what happens as the Owl and the Pussy-Cat sail away in their beautiful pea-green boat!

Song of the North
Frank Asch, Author
Ted Levin, Photographer
San Diego: Gulliver Green/Harcourt. 1999. 0-15-201258-3.

This poem tells of creatures that live in the north. Photographs show the animals in their natural habitats, and a listing of all of the animals in the poem is included in the back of the book.

Without Wings, Mother, How Can I Fly?
Norma Farber, Author
Keiko Narahashi, Illustrator
New York: Holt. 1998. 0-8050-3380-7.

Like most children, the boy in this story has many questions about how he could perform the same actions that are performed by animals. Through the questions he poses and the answers his mother gives him, the boy discovers that using his imagination to see things a little differently will enable him to do anything he wants to do. The accompanying watercolor illustrations add a comforting feel to the text.

 Focus on Phonological Awareness (initial sound substitution): During a second reading of the book, point out to children that the author has changed the beginning sound(s) to create words that rhyme.

Collections

Alligators and Others All Year Long: A Book of Months
Crescent Dragonwagon, Author
Jose Aruego and Ariane Dewey, Illustrators
New York: Aladdin. 1997. 0-689-81554-9.

In poetic form, each of the animals in this text celebrates the months of the year. Each month also depicts a related present. The months and the presents for each are compiled in the back of the book.

Alphabestiary: Animal Poems from A to Z
Jane Yolen, Collector
Allan Eitzen, Illustrator
Honesdale, PA: Wordsong/Boyds Mills. 1995. 1-56397-222-0.

Here is a volume that provides seventy-one poems about animals, some for each letter of the alphabet, written by poets such as William Blake, Aileen

Fisher, and Christina Rossetti. The poems are short and lively, making them enjoyable listening or reading experiences for children. Celebrate the many animals that inhabit the earth through the reading of these delightful poems. Watercolor and cut-paper illustrations provide visions of the many animals presented throughout the text.

Animals That Ought to Be: Poems About Imaginary Animals
Richard Michelson, Author
Leonard Baskin, Illustrator
New York: Simon & Schuster. 1996. 0-689-80635-3.

Imagine a new animal. What would it look like? How would it behave? This collection of poems presents several imaginary animals to get you started! Meet Nightlight Bird who chases away shadows. Meet Leftover Eater who eats more than leftovers! The watercolor illustrations depict the imaginary animal presented in each poem.

☐ *Book Extender:* Invite children to construct their own imaginary animals. Divide the class, instructing each child in one half to draw the head and top half of the body of an animal and each child in the other half to draw the hind end of an animal. Then pair heads and tails and have them create a name and a verse for their animal.

Asana and the Animals: A Book of Pet Poems
Grace Nichols, Author
Sarah Adams, Illustrator
Cambridge, MA: Candlewick. 1997. 0-7636-0145-4.

From a poem about a parrot to one about a giraffe, here is a collection of poems in which a little girl describes many different animals. Children are sure to identify with some of the animals described in the poems.

B Is for Baby: An Alphabet of Verses
Myra Cohn Livingston, Author
Steel Stillman, Photographer
New York: McElderry/Simon & Schuster. 1996. 0-689-80950-6.

These short poems celebrate the many moods and actions of babies. Each poem stands alone; however, read together, the poems create a book that reflects the many actions and reactions of babies from A to Z. The photographs depict babies from different cultural groups, making this book an excellent means of helping children see the likenesses among different cultures.

Beastly Banquet
Peggy Munsterberg, Author
Tracy Gallup, Illustrator
New York: Dial/Penguin. 1997. 0-8037-1481-5.

This collection of animal poems tells about the eating habits of many different animals. Each short, lively poem is embedded in a watercolor illustration that shows the animal feeding on what it likes best. The poems can be read as individual poems or as a group.

📖 *Book Extender:* Before reading this collection, develop a chart that has two columns. At the top of one column write "Animal." On the top of the second column, write "Eats." Gather the children in front of the chart and tell them that all the poems you will be reading today tell about animals and what they like to eat. As you are reading, you want them to listen for the name of the animal and what the animal likes to eat. After each poem, invite students to share their responses as you or a student recorder writes them in the appropriate places on the chart. This chart can serve as a review once all the poems have been read.

The Bookworm's Feast: A Potluck of Poems
J. Patrick Lewis, Author
John O'Brien, Illustrator
New York: Dial. 1999. 0-8037-1692-3.

This is no ordinary collection of poems! It features poems on many different topics, and they are organized into categories according to the courses of a royal feast. From appetizers to delectable desserts, the poems provide quite a feast!

Candy Corn
James Stevenson, Author and Illustrator
New York: Greenwillow. 1999. 0-688-15837-4.

This is the compilation of twenty-four short poems on a variety of subjects. They are perfect short reads that provide a variety of language play.

A Child's Calendar
John Updike, Author
Trina Schart Hyman, Illustrator
New York: Holiday House. 1999. 0-8234-1445-0.

From January through December, Updike provides one poem for each month of the year. But this book is about so much more! The illustration for each poem shows interracial interactions, helping children to see that regardless of their race, all people are alike in some ways.

Climb into My Lap: First Poems to Read Together
Lee Bennett Hopkins, Compiler
Kathryn Brown, Illustrator
New York: Simon & Schuster. 1998. 0-689-80715-5.

Here is a vast collection of poetry that is sure to be enjoyed by all. Hopkins has assembled a balance of poems intended as read-alouds, in terms of both the represented poets and the variety of the poems themselves. All poems are classified into one of eight categories ranging from those that focus on "Me" to those that are perfect for "Good Night." The watercolor illustrations enhance the collection and invite listeners into the poems.

Doodle Dandies: Poems That Take Shape
J. Patrick Lewis, Author
Lisa Desimini, Illustrator
New York: Atheneum/Simon & Schuster. 1998. 0-689-81075-X.

Words actually take shape in this collection of shape poems. Each poem is written to represent the shape of the subject it addresses. From *giraffe* to *skyscraper*, children will take delight in the many ways letters and words are used to create images.

📖 *Book Extender:* Invite children to make their own shape poems.

Elephants and Emus: and Other Animal Rhymes
Philippa-Alys Browne, Compiler and Illustrator
Watertown, MA: Charlesbridge. 1997. 0-88106-698-2.

The poems in this collection represent an array of animals and read as a whole may make the listener feel as though he or she is on safari. The poems are drawn from several different poets, providing a nice collection of animal rhymes.

Elephant Games and Other Playful Poems to Perform
Brod Bagert, Author
Tim Ellis, Illustrator
Honesdale, PA: Boyds Mills. 1995. 1-56397-293-X.

Here is a collection of poems that invites children to perform. From "Elephant Games" to "The Life Song," Bagert capitalizes on lines that rhyme to create poems that are both humorous and thoughtful. Watercolor and colored-pencil illustrations accompany each poem, providing readers with an image conveyed by the words.

📖 *Book Extender:* Most of the poems in this collection invite student participation. Invite students to perform as you read the poems aloud.

Families: Poems Celebrating the African American Experience
Dorothy S. Strickland and Michael R. Strickland, Compilers
John Ward, Illustrator
Honesdale, PA: Boyds Mills Press. 1994. 1-56397-288-3.

What does it mean to be a family? The poems in this volume answer this most important question. Poets such as Langston Hughes, Eloise Greenfield, and Nikki Giovanni offer their perspectives on family life through the short, concise poems they share. Acrylic illustrations help the reader celebrate the diversity of African American families, leading them to celebrate their own as well.

📖 *Book Extender:* Provide time for students to tell about significant events in their families.

Flicker Flash
Joan Bransfield Graham, Author
Nancy Davis, Illustrator
Boston: Houghton Mifflin. 1999. 0-395-90501-X.

Light illuminates our lives, as this collection of poems illustrates. Each poem shows one way that light serves the world. Taken together, the poems help us see just how important light is in our everyday lives. Each poem is formatted so that it takes on the shape of the object shedding the light.

Gimme a Break, Rattlesnake!
Sonja Dunn, Compiler
Mark Thurman, Illustrator
Toronto, Canada: Stoddart. 1994. 0-7737-5696-5.

Here is a collection of favorite schoolyard chants and some other short poems that invite language play through the use of both rhyme and rhythm. Many of the chants are short enough for students to memorize and are perfect for those few minutes before or after school.

A Helpful Alphabet of Friendly Objects
John Updike, Author
David Updike, Photographer
New York: Knopf. 1995. 0-679-84324-8.

Common objects for every letter of the alphabet form the basis for the poems in this collection. Each poem is accompanied by a photograph that shows the object in its environment.

 Focus on Phonological Awareness (word): To further children's understanding that words represent objects, place letters of the alphabet into a paper bag. In turn, invite volunteers to draw a letter out of the bag. Students then name the object in the poem that corresponds with the selected letter.

Home on the Range: Cowboy Poetry
Paul B. Janeczko, Compiler
Bernie Fuchs, Illustrator
New York: Dial/Penguin. 1997. 0-8037-1910-8.

Use these twenty poems to help you imagine what it would be like to ride with 1,000 cattle, to share a campfire meal with a friend, and to spend the

night sleeping under the stars. Each poem, with its accompanying pencil-
and-oil illustration, helps create a sense of different aspects of cowboy life.
From short four-line poems to full-page poems, each contributes to a volume that captures the cowboy's heroic spirit.

How Now, Brown Cow?
Alice Schertle, Author
Amanda Schaffer, Illustrator
San Diego: Browndeer/Harcourt Brace. 1994. 0-15-276648-0.

Want to know what cows really think as they are grazing in the pasture?
These poems let you know! These short, funny poems, which are accompanied by full-page oil paintings, invite readers and listeners to imagine
what cows would tell us if they could speak.

I Am the Cat
Alice Shertle, Author
Mark Buehner, Illustrator
New York: Lothrop. 1999. 0-688-13153-0.

We all know that cats have minds of their own and that they are independent creatures. The poems in this collection provide a glimpse into what
cats might actually be thinking as they romp in the grass and rub up against
their owners' ankles.

I Never Did That Before
Lilian Moore, Author
Lillian Hoban, Illustrator
New York: Atheneum/Simon & Schuster. 1995. 0-689-31889-8.

The joys of doing something new and the new discoveries and feelings of
accomplishment that result are the focus of these short poems. All children
are sure to relate to the common childhood experiences these poems express. Breaking in new sneakers, overcoming a fear of the dark, learning to
greet a person in a different language, and growing out of a favorite coat are
a few of the many adventures played out in these poems. Hoban's illustrations bring the experiences to life.

📖 *Book Extender:* After children listen to several of these poems, they are sure to want to tell about one of their "firsts." Provide time for them to do just that. To show students how writing can be used to record information, you might want to record each student's name and his or her "first" next to it.

In the Swim
Douglas Florian, Author and Illustrator
San Diego: Harcourt Brace. 1997. 0-15-201307-5.

Here are twenty-one poems about underwater creatures that are sure to capture the interest of readers of all ages. From piranhas to the tetra, readers will experience a collection of humorous poems composed of short lines that invite participation.

It's About Time!
Florence Heide, Judith Gilliand, and Roxanne Pierce, Authors
Cathryn Falwell, Illustrator
New York: Clarion. 1999. 0-395-86612-X.

Time can be a difficult concept for children to grasp, partly because the word is used in many different contexts, making it take on different meanings. Here is a collection of sixteen poems that help children better understand time — telling time as well as other meanings of the word.

Jumpety-Bumpety Hop: A Parade of Animal Poems
Kay Charao, Compiler and Illustrator
New York: Dutton. 1997. 0-525-45825-5.

Many different animals are represented in this collection of poems written by both English and American poets. Favorite rhymes such as "Monkeys on the Bed" and poems by such notable poets as William Wordsworth work together to create all kinds of poems for all ages of readers. The illustrations help the reader visualize the animals in action.

Laugh-Eteria
Douglas Florian, Author and Illustrator
San Diego: Harcourt. 1999. 0-15-202084-5.

If you want a good laugh, you need this book! It is the compilation of more than 150 humorous poems that can be read in any order. The poems address many topics including school, trees, and hair.

Lemonade Sun and Other Summer Poems
Rebecca Kai Dotlich, Author
Jan Spivey Gilchrist, Illustrator
Honesdale, PA: Wordsong/Boyds Mills. 1998. 1-56397-660-9.

Summer brings many delights, many of which are expressed in the poems that compose this book. From lemonade on hot days to fireworks on the Fourth of July, children will relate to the sights and sounds portrayed in these short, descriptive poems. At times, the acrylic illustrations feature the underlying message for more than one poem.

📖 *Book Extender:* To teach children about themes, conceal the cover of the book and invite children to listen to several of the poems. Then ask them to tell how all the poems are alike—how they relate to one another—and to provide their reasons. Once the discussion has concluded, reveal the cover of the book to see if any theme they identified is similar to the actual title.

The Little Buggers: Insect and Spider Poems
J. Patrick Lewis, Author
Victoria Chess, Illustrator
New York: Dial/Penguin. 1998. 0-8037-1769-5.

Vivid watercolor illustrations of insects and spiders add a visual dimension to the poems that compose this volume. Everything from termites to doodlebugs are represented, and children are sure to squirm with joy as they read or listen to the short, descriptive verses. While all descriptions are true to the respective insect or spider, they are depicted in fun scenarios. They can be enjoyed as an entire collection or as single poems.

Little Dog Poems
Kristine O'Connell George, Author
June Otani, Illustrator
New York: Clarion. 1999. 0-395-82266-1.

What do dogs do to fill up their days? The short poems in this collection answer this question. From morning until bedtime, dogs perform many useful functions!

📖 *Book Extender:* Children who have dogs as pets are sure to want to talk about them after they hear some or all of the poems in this text. Provide time for them to do so.

The Llama Who Had No Pajama: 100 Favorite Poems
Mary Ann Hoberman, Author
Betty Fraser, Illustrator
San Diego: Bowdner Press/Harcourt Brace. 1998. 0-15-200111-5.

Forty years in the making, this collection of poems represents some of the best by Hoberman. Many subjects are represented, from animals to growing. Many of these poems are short, funny, and playful. Indeed, they invite language play at its best. The detailed illustrations are sprinkled throughout, making this an excellent volume of poetry for beginners.

Love's a Sweet
Clyde Watson, Author
Wendy Watson, Illustrator
New York: Viking/Penguin. 1998. 0-670-83453-X.

The ups and downs of love in commonplace situations are explored in this collection of short poems illustrated with animal characters. Children are sure to relate to one or more of these verses.

Make Things Fly: Poems About the Wind
Dorothy M. Kennedy, Editor
Sasha Meret, Illustrator
New York: McElderry/Simon & Schuster. 1998. 0-689-81544-1.

What does the wind look like? How does it feel? How does it move? How does it affect objects that it touches? The poems in this volume answer these questions and more. Accompanied by line drawings, the words used to create the poems help the reader or listener sense the power of wind.

Old Elm Speaks: Tree Poems
Kristine O'Connell George, Author
Kate Kiesler, Illustrator
New York: Clarion. 1998. 0-395-87611-7.

This book represents a collection of poems about trees. However, what makes these poems unique is that most of the trees take on personalities and tell the story from their own perspective.

On the Wing: Bird Poems and Paintings
Douglas Florian, Author and Illustrator
San Diego: Harcourt Brace. 1996. 0-15-200497-1.

This collection of twenty-one bird poems is sure to delight those who are interested in birds. Florian uses few yet powerful words to describe the birds in short verselike poems. A full-page watercolor painting shows the bird being described in each poem.

Once in the Country: Poems of a Farm
Tony Johnston, Author
Thomas Allen, Illustrator
New York: Putnam. 1996. 0-399-22644-3.

What is it like to live in the country during the different seasons? What are the secrets and treasures of living in the country? The poems in this collection answer these questions. Written as a collection that tells the story of country life, the poems can also be enjoyed as stand-alones. Each poem is no longer than one page. The carefully chosen text and the pastel illustrations used to provide images of the ideas represented in the poems make them accessible to many readers.

Riddle Road: Puzzles in Poems and Pictures
Elizabeth Spires, Author
Erik Blegvad, Illustrator
New York: McElderry/Simon & Schuster. 1999. 0-689-81783-5.

This collection of twenty-six riddles is a little different. Each riddle provides information about an object, and clues are provided in the accompanying illustrations. Once students take a guess, turn the book upside down to reveal the correct answer!

Sawgrass Poems: A View of the Everglades
Frank Asch, Author
Ted Levin, Photographer
San Diego: Gulliver Green/Harcourt Brace. 1996. 0-15-200180-8.

The poems and their accompanying photographs are assembled to provide insight into the many forms of life that make up the ecosystem known as the Florida Everglades. Levin's introduction provides background about the Everglades—how it came to be and what threatens it. His detailed photographs provide vivid images that coincide with Asch's poems. Notes and photo captions at the end of the book provide interested readers with additional information about the life forms presented in the poems, making this an excellent book to weave together poetry and nonfiction. Whether the poems are read as a collection or as individual poems, children are sure to delight in discovering the many life forms that exist in this wetland.

School Supplies: A Book of Poems
Lee Bennett Hopkins, Compiler
Renee Flower, Illustrator
New York: Simon & Schuster. 1996. 0-689-80497-0.

Take a look at school supplies through poetry lenses! This collection enables you to do just that. Poems are provided for school supplies such as paper clips, pencils, and pens. Taken as a whole, the poems tell a story of children as they begin their school day on the bus and use the necessary supplies to complete their schoolwork throughout the day. Vibrant watercolor and colored pencil drawings are used to bring the poems to life. Children will be enticed to say or write poems about their own school supplies after hearing or reading these poems.

📖 *Book Extender:* Put several school supplies in a large paper bag. Invite a student to select an item as the rest of the class creates an oral or written verse to go with it.

118

Sleep Rhymes Around the World
Jane Yolen, Editor
Illustrated by Seventeen International Artists
Honesdale, PA: Wordsong/Boyds Mills. 1994. 1-56397-243-3.

Bedtime happens to everyone all over the world as do the bedtime rhymes that are featured in this collection. In all, seventeen different nations are represented through the lullabies, which are illustrated by an artist from each country and are written both in the language of that nation and in English. These short lullabies serve as good reminders that while we are different, we are also alike.

Spectacular Science: A Book of Poems
Lee Bennett Hopkins, Compiler
Virginia Halstead, Illustrator
New York: Simon & Schuster. 1999. 0-689-81283-3.

These poems provide students with answers and questions about science-related topics. A variety of poets provide either explanations of scientific happenings or questions that spark wonder.

A Stitch in Rhyme
Belinda Downers, Compiler and Illustrator
New York: Knopf. 1996. 0-679-97679-5.

Presented here is a collection of forty-eight familiar rhymes such as "Jack and Jill," "This Little Piggy," and "Hey, Diddle, Diddle." Downers provides embroidered illustrations for each, making them warm and inviting. A border surrounds each page.

📖 *Book Extender:* After children have listened to or read these rhymes, invite them to share some of their favorite rhymes.

Street Rhymes Around the World
Jane Yolen, Editor
Illustrated by Seventeen International Artists
Honesdale, PA: Wordsong/Boyds Mills. 1992. 1-878093-53-3.

This collection includes street rhymes from seventeen nations and repub-
lics. What is especially intriguing about it is that each rhyme is printed in
its original language as well as in an English translation.

Snow, Snow: Winter Poems for Children
Jane Yolen, Author
Jason Stemple, Photographer
Honesdale, PA: Wordsong/Boyds Mills. 1998. 1-56397-721-4.

The wonders of snow—how it looks and feels, activities that can happen
in it, and the effect it has on our surroundings—is the subject of this collection. The photographs capture the beauty of snow as it dresses the out-
doors with its crystals. The short poems about common experiences in snow
are sure to invite children to reflect on their own experiences.

Song and Dance
Lee Bennett Hopkins, Compiler
Cheryl Munro Taylor, Illustrator
New York: Simon & Schuster. 1997. 0-689-80159-9.

The poems in this volume tell of song or dance. They remind us that music is all around us any time of the day. Hand-cut, hand-colored, and hand-
made papers were used to create the vibrant illustrations that seem to move
with the words of the poems. From rap to jazz, readers and listeners are sure
to catch the beat!

Splish Splash
Joan Bransfield Graham, Author
Steve Scott, Illustrator
New York: Ticknor & Fields. 1994. 0-395-70128-7.

Water can take on many forms as the poems in this volume show. Each
poem conveys a different water form and is accompanied by an illustration
that reflects the water in this form, making the poems very concrete for
youngsters. From ice cubes to the ocean, the poems are sure to provide listeners with a sense of playing with words and the shapes they portray—
the shapes of language!

📖 *Book Extender:* Brainstorm other words that suggest images and invite children to create a visual image using the letters of the word just as Graham does in this collection of poems.

Sweets and Treats
Bobbye S. Goldstein, Compiler
Kathy Couri, Illustrator
New York: Hyperion. 1998. 0-7868-1280-X.

Any person who likes desserts will enjoy the poems that compose this volume. Like desserts that have fruit? Read the poems that are topped off with fruit. Like ice cream instead? Read the many poems about this delicious sweet. Of course some children like cookies, candy, cake, and other sweet snacks, and there are poems for these treats, too. Poets such as Eve Mirriam, Karla Kuskin, and Shel Silverstein provide a wealth of poems that can be read to, with, or by youngsters.

📖 *Book Extender:* Children are sure to want to tell about their favorite treats. Construct a semantic map of their favorites.

Tea Party Today: Poems to Sip and Savor
Eileen Spinelli, Author
Karen Dugan, Illustrator
Honesdale, PA: Wordsong/Boyds Mills. 1999. 1-56397-662-5.

This collection of poems invites listeners to several tea parties and offers tips for those who want to have their own. Recipes for making different kinds of tea are also included. As a result of experiencing this collection of poetry, listeners will have a new, broadened perspective on what it means to have a successful tea party.

This Big Sky
Pat Mora, Author
Steve Jenkins, Illustrator
New York: Scholastic. 1998. 0-590-37120-7.

The landscape, people, and animals of the American Southwest are described in this collection of fourteen lyrical poems. Spanish is sometimes used and a glossary giving the pronunciation and English translation is provided. Jenkins' cut-paper illustrations provide images of the Southwest and evoke feelings of a vast, powerful place that is big enough for everyone's dreams.

Truck Talk: Rhymes on Wheels
Bobbi Katz, Author
Photographs by others
New York: Scholastic. 1997. 0-590-69328-X.

What would happen if trucks could talk? What would they tell us? This collection of poems gives us some possible answers. Each poem highlights a different truck, which talks about what it does and what it likes.

Very Best (Almost) Friends: Poems of Friendship
Paul Janeczko, Compiler
Christine Daveneir, Illustrator
Cambridge, MA: Candlewick. 1999. 0-7636-0475-5.

This collection of twenty-four poems by children's favorite poets—such as Walter Dean Myers, Myra Cohn Livingston, and Lois Lenski—focuses on friendship. The poems explore both the ups and the downs of friendships, offering children a realistic picture of what it means to have meaningful relationships with others. Watercolor and pen-and-ink illustrations capture the poets' intended meanings.

Water Music
Jane Yolen, Author
Jason Stemple, Illustrator
Honesdale, PA: Wordsong/Boyds Mills. 1995. 1-56397-336-7.

How does water feel? What emotions does it evoke? The poems in this volume, along with the photographs that inspired them, answer questions like these. While waterfalls are sure to evoke a sense of awe and wonderment, soap bubbles conjure up other feelings. Taken together, the concise, descriptive poems invite the reader or listener to revisit a basic element of life that is sometimes taken for granted.

Weird Pet Poems
Dilys Evans, Compiler
Jacqueline Rogers, Illustrator
New York: Simon & Schuster. 1997. 0-689-80734-1.

Who can resist these poems about unusual pets by poets such as Karla Kus-kin and Lee Bennett Hopkins? These poems invite children to use their imagination as they explore happenings, both real and imaginary, with these unusual pets. Taken together, the poems tell of an eight-year-old boy's quest for the perfect pet. The imaginative watercolor illustrations leave much for children to discover.

Where Go the Boats?
Robert Louis Stevenson, Author
Max Grover, Illustrator
San Diego: Harcourt. 1998. 0-15-201711-9.

This is a collection of four of Robert Lewis Stevenson's best-loved poems for children. Each poem invites listeners to actually create what is being mentioned in the verse(s) of the poem.

📖 *Book Extender:* This text cries out for dramatization! Have students pantomime the various lines that are mentioned in each verse. Of course, props can also be used if they are available.

With One White Wing: Puzzles in Poems and Pictures
Elizabeth Spires, Author
Erik Blegvad, Illustrator
New York: McElderry/Simon & Schuster. 1995. 0-689-50622-8.

Readers and listeners are invited to put clues together to determine what is being described in each riddle presented in this book. The illustrations also provide clues as they show the object somewhere in the picture. An-swers are provided at the bottom of the page, printed upside down. These short, descriptive riddles are sure to engage readers or listeners as they try to solve the twenty-one puzzles.

📖 *Book Extender:* This is an excellent book for showing children how to use the author's words to construct meaning from the text. After reading each line, talk about what the clues convey to show students how to identify the clues and how to put them together. For example, using the first poem on page 7, you might say something like this:

Read the first line of the poem that tells about two hands holding an object.
"Hmmm," you say. "I need two hands to hold this object."

Read the second line of the poem about feet avoiding the object.
"I use two hands to hold it, but I don't want my feet to touch it."

Read the last two lines of the poem and say something such as:
"So this is something I hold but have to jump over or I'll fall down. I wonder if the picture can give me any help. Yes! I see someone using a jump rope. I'll guess jump rope."

6

Song Texts

Singing is a part of youngsters' everyday lives. They sing as they play, clean up, and get ready for bed. And whether or not they realize it, their use of song enables them to discover much about the sound structure of their language. Many songs, for example, use rhyme. Sometimes the rhyme is created by changing the beginning sounds (e.g., *hen, pen*), other times by adding an initial sound (e.g., *top, stop*). At still other times, the rhyme is created by using different spellings to (e.g., *bright, white*). Regardless of how the rhyme is created, children's attention is naturally drawn to this language feature as they listen to and sing the song.

Teachers can also highlight a specific language feature by drawing children's attention to it. The teacher who comments, "*Ho, go*—they rhyme!" is helping children become aware of rhyming. Gradually, then, children begin to see that sounds in words can be manipulated, creating new words and messages along the way. Indeed, using songs to further nurture phonological awareness in general—and phonemic awareness in particular—is a logical and meaningful extension of children's everyday lives.

Following is a list of three ways that songs are often used to enhance phonological awareness. All are of value; however, the emphasis in this book in general, and this chapter in particular, is on using children's literature.

1. Use the tune of familiar songs such as "Old MacDonald Had a Farm" to create verses that focus on specific phonemic awareness tasks. Yopp (1992) suggests several songs as does Eldredge (1995). Say, for instance, that you want to help the children focus on sound isolation and you want

to use the song "Old MacDonald" as a vehicle. You create the following verse and invite children to participate in the singing:

> What's the sound that starts these words:
> *mat, men, moo?*
> (Pause for student response)
> /m/ is the sound that starts these words:
> *mat, men, moo*
> With a /m/, /m/, here, and a /m/, /m/ there,
> Here a /m/, there a /m/, everywhere a /m/, /m/
> /m/ is the sound that starts these words,
> *mat, men, moo.*
> (Based on Yopp 1992).

2. Look at the lyrics of original songs written for children to see which, if any, lend themselves to specific phonemic-awareness tasks shown on page 7. Yopp and Yopp (1997) have done just that in their volume entitled *Oo-pples and Boo-noo-noos*, providing the musical score for each, too. One of the forty songs they provide is "Bibbidi-Bobbidi-Boo" from Walt Disney's *Cinderella*. A close look at the lyrics shows that the song is a natural for calling attention to alliteration, phoneme substitution, and phoneme manipulation (see page 7 for a review of these terms).

3. Use song-picture books (i.e., picture books that have been created to illustrate a given song, such as "Mockingbird"). In this way, children develop an understanding of the oral language aspect of their language. They also see it written in a text, which helps them discover that songs can be put in a written form and that they are another way of communicating ideas with others. The song-picture books shown in this chapter are the most recently published examples of this genre. They also have the potential to make the transition to reading an effortless and enjoyable experience; children know the lyrics so well they can't help but read the words! A positive attitude about reading results.

————————◆————————

A-Hunting We Will Go!
Steven Kellogg, Author and Illustrator
New York: Morrow. 1998. 0-688-14944-8.

Based on the traditional refrain, this song tells the story of a crew that has no intention of doing what they are supposed to do—go to sleep. Instead, they gather their animal friends and take off on an adventure that takes them to a place where the sun doesn't set until the kids want it to. After the fun, the children land in bed and are soon fast asleep. The musical score is included in the back of the text.

📖 *Book Extender:* Invite children to create their own verses that can be sung to this traditional folk song. The verses could relate to different tasks at school.

All the Pretty Little Horses
Linda Saport, Illustrator
New York: Clarion. 1999. 0-395-93097-9.

Pastels are used to illustrate this traditional rhyme. Two lines of the song appear on each two-page spread, making the book an inviting read or sing. A note from Saport offering background about the song opens the book. She also provides the musical score in the back of the book.

Animal Music
Harriet Ziefert, Author
Donald Saaf, Illustrator
Boston: Houghton Mifflin. 1999. 0-395-95294-8.

In this rhythmical text, many different animals play musical instruments as they march along. Listeners will have a hard time sitting still as they hear and see what the animals do.

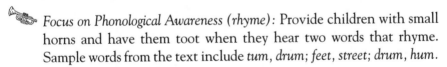 *Focus on Phonological Awareness (rhyme):* Provide children with small horns and have them toot when they hear two words that rhyme. Sample words from the text include *tum, drum; feet, street; drum, hum.*

📖 *Book Extender:* Encourage children to create their own band after listening to this story. Provide them with musical instruments and take them out to the playground for their marching band parade.

The Baby Chicks Sing
Nancy Abraham Hall and Jill Syverson-Stork, Compilers and
  Adapters
Kay Chorao, Illustrator
New York: Little, Brown. 1994. 0-316-33852-4.

Here is a collection of games, nursery rhymes, and songs from Spanish-speaking countries. Musical scores are included with the songs, and every part of the text is written in both Spanish and English. Taken together, this collection provides a glimpse into other cultures while celebrating the common bonds among children.

Barnyard Lullaby
Frank Asch, Author and Illustrator
Melissa Chesnut, Composer
New York: Simon & Schuster. 1998. 0-689-81363-5.

What sounds like music to one person can sound like noise to another! Such is the case in this text. As each mother animal sings her baby a lullaby, the baby is comforted and loves her song, whereas all the farmer hears is noise. In the end, the farmer's wife sings their baby to sleep, which lulls both the baby and the farmer to sleep, but all the animals hear is noise! Music is included in the back of the text.

📖 *Book Extender:* Divide children into seven groups. Each group can learn one verse to sing and sing it in turn when the class performs the song. The entire class can sing the chorus.

Big Jim and the White-Legged Moose
Jim Arnovsky, Author and Illustrator
New York: Lothrop. 1999. 0-688-10864-4.

As Arnovsky tells readers in the back of the book, this song is based on his encounter with a large moose ten years ago. In it, he tells how he follows the trail of a big moose to get a good sketch of it. That is, of course, until the moose makes him drop his sketch book and other supplies in order to climb to a safe place. The musical score is included in both the front and back of the book.

Down by the Station
Will Hillenbrand, Author and Illustrator
San Diego: Harcourt. 1999. 0-15-201804-2.

Come join the fun by singing along as different animals get on the train to ride to the children's zoo! The repetitive verse will encourage children to

128

sing along as each animal boards the train. The musical score is provided in the back of the text.

📖 *Book Extender:* Place pictures of animals shown in the book in a bag, making sure that you have enough pictures so that each child can participate. In turn, ask children to select a picture from the bag. When singing the song through a second or third time, have children make the sound of the animal they selected when the animal boards the train. Children could be assigned to different animals and could give their sounds in progression like the animals in the book. Finally, use the children's names when singing the verses.

Engine, Engine, Number Nine
Stephanie Calmenson, Author
Paul Meisel, Illustrator
New York: Hyperion. 1996. 0-7868-2127-2.

In this story (song), a train makes several stops before reaching its final destination, picking up many passengers along the way. So sing along as you board the train. Toot! Toot!

The Farmer in the Dell
Alexandra Wallner, Illustrator
New York: Holiday House. 1998. 0-8234-1382-9.

Here is an illustrated form of the traditional song loved by many. The music, along with accompanying verses, is provided in the back of the text.

📖 *Book Extender:* Have different children take on the role of different characters in the story and act it out as it is sung.

Farmyard Song
Carol Morley, Author and Illustrator
New York: Simon & Schuster. 1994. 0-671-89551-6.

In this much-loved song, children learn about different animals and sounds associated with them, from the hen who goes "chimmy-chuck, chimmy-chuck" to the dog who goes "bow-wow, bow-wow." The cat has the last words: "fiddle-I-fee."

Focus on Phonological Awareness (phoneme substitution): After each verse, have children change the beginning sound to help the cat say something different each time. Thus, "fiddle-I-fee" becomes "biddle-I-bee" and so on.

Frog Went A-Courting: A Musical Play in Six Acts
Dominic Catalano, Reteller and Illustrator
Honesdale, PA: Boyds Mills. 1998. 1-56397-637-4.

In the retelling of this traditional folk song, a frog courts and eventually marries a mouse with the Reverend Bug presiding over the ceremony. All is fine until a tomcat makes an unwelcome appearance. All ends well, though, as the cat puts a stop to Frog's music by chomping on his bagpipes while Frog and Mouse go off to France. Music is included in the back of the book.

Going to the Zoo
Tom Paxton, Author
Karen Lee Schmidt, Illustrator
New York: Morrow. 1996. 0-688-13800-4.

Daddy's taking everybody to the zoo, and you can come along, too! Join in the fun as you sing your way to and in the zoo, looking at the many different animals. A musical score is included in both the front and back of the book.

Halley Came to Jackson
Mary Carpenter, Author
Dan Andreasen, Illustrator
New York: HarperCollins. 1998. 0-06-025400-9.

This is a picture-book version of the song that Mary Carpenter wrote in which she sings about the night in 1910 when Halley's Comet zoomed across the sky. The song was inspired by Eudora Welty's family story, which tells about how her father took baby Eudora to the window to watch the comet. While the actual music is not shown, a cassette tape that features Carpenter singing the song is included with the book.

Hey, Little Ant
Phillip and Hannah Hoose, Authors
Debbie Tilley, Illustrator
Berkeley: Tricycle. 1998. 1-883672-54-6.

A young boy starts to stomp on an ant but stops when the ant looks up at him and starts talking. In this song, the boy and the ant have a conversation leading the boy—and others who experience this text—to ponder, "Should I quish or shouldn't I?" The musical score and accompanying verses are shown in the back of the text.

📖 *Book Extender:* This book is set up as a conversation between the boy and the ant and is formatted accordingly (like play format). Pair students and have one take on the role of the boy and the other read the part of the ant. A follow-up discussion focused on respecting and valuing all life forms is a natural.

Hush, Little Alien
Daniel Kirk, Author and Illustrator
New York: Hyperion. 1999. 0-7868-0538-2.

Here is an adaptation of "Hush, Little Baby," a familiar lullaby. In this version, an extraterrestrial child is promised several outer-space presents, including a kiss from his father.

📖 *Book Extender:* Invite children to innovate on this song by generating another person or animal that could "hush" along with different presents used to do so.

Hush, Little Baby
Marla Frazee, Illustrator
San Diego: Browndeer/Harcourt. 1999. 0-15-201429-2.

True to the original song, the baby is crying and others are trying to comfort it by giving it presents. What makes the story take on a new feel are the updated illustrations. The baby does stop crying, but is it the presents or being tired that makes this happen? Sing the song, look at the pictures. You be the judge!

Focus on Phonological Awareness (word): The large print shown on the bottom of each page makes this a very good book for helping children develop the concept of word. During a second reading or singing of the book, frame each word with your hands or a card so students can see where words begin and end.

I've Been Working on the Railroad: An American Classic
Nadine Bernard Westcott, Illustrator
New York: Hyperion. 1996. 0-7868-0053-4.

In this updated take on the traditional song, a young boy arrives at the train station a little early and gets rewarded for doing so. When he boards the train, he gets to ride up front with the conductor! Come discover who's in the kitchen with Dinah! A musical score is included in the back of the book as is a brief historical sketch of the song.

The Jungle Baseball Game
Tom Paxton, Author
Karen Lee Schmidt, Illustrator
New York: Morrow. 1999. 0-688-13979-5.

Can the hippos beat the monkeys and win this baseball game? The monkeys don't think so, at least at the beginning of the game. But then the hippos decide that they want to win and will let nothing get in their way. The book is based on the song by the same title, and the musical score is included in both the front and back of the book.

Little Factory
Sarah Weeks, Author and Singer
Bryon Barton, Illustrator and Animator
Michael Abbott, Composer
New York: HarperCollins. 1998. 0-06-027429-8.

This song tells the story of a little man who runs one little factory that is very profitable. All is well until the little man is told to expand the factory. After the expansion is complete, the pollution drives workers away, and the little man solves the problem by tearing down the large factory, and building a little one powered by the sun. The workers return and all ends well. This book is accompanied by a CD-ROM that provides many options for the reader or listener. The book can be heard with the music and the animation can be viewed, it can be read to the child, or the child can read along. The youngster can also click on any one line of text and it will be read to him or her.

Lucky Song
Vera B. Williams, Author and Illustrator
New York: Greenwillow. 1997. 0-688-14459-4.

Little Evie is the main character in this story, and she wants to do something. Each succeeding page leads us to her doing something: flying a kite. She then returns home, has dinner, goes to bed, only to wake up wanting to repeat the process.

Lullaby Raft
Naomi Shihab Nye, Author
Vivienne Flesher, Illustrator
New York: Simon & Schuster. 1997. 0-689-80521-7.

As the sun goes down, different mother animals sing their youngsters a lullaby to put them to sleep. The musical score is included in the back of the book with accompanying verses shown below it.

Mary Had a Little Lamb
Sarah Josepha Hale, Author
Salley Mavor, Illustrator
New York: Orchard. 1995. 0-531-06875-7.

We all know what happens when Mary's lamb follows her to school, but do we really know what the lamb looked like? These fabric-relief illustrations provide one view while breathing a whole new life into this familiar song. The history of the song is included in the back of the book.

Mockingbird
Allan Ahlberg, Author
Paul Howard, Illustrator
Cambridge, MA: Candlewick. 1998. 0-7636-0439-9.

This is a variation of the original lullaby, which, like the original, promises a baby a variety of presents from various people.

📖 *Book Extender:* Pass out pictures of the various objects shown in the book. In turn, have children place their picture in the pocket holder in the same order as the objects are mentioned in the text. Use the text to verify.

Ms. MacDonald Has a Class
Jan Ormerod, Author and Illustrator
New York: Clarion. 1996. 0-395-77611-2.

After they visit a farm, the children in Ms. MacDonald's class create different movements as they prepare for a class play to be performed for parents. Children will sing along as they are familiar with the tune, which is taken from "Old MacDonald Had a Farm."

No Mirrors in My Nana's House
Ysaye M. Barnwell, Author
Synthia Saint James, Illustrator
San Diego: Harcourt. 1998. 0-15-201825-5.

The message of this song is a powerful one: no mirrors can be used to determine the inner beauty of any individual. Instead, we can often discover this beauty by interacting with others. In this case, the girl discovers her inner beauty by looking into her Nana's eyes. A CD-ROM is included with this book so that students can hear the author reading the text as a musical group sings the song.

Old MacDonald
Amy Schwartz, Illustrator
New York: Scholastic. 1999. 0-590-46189-3.

Here's yet another version of the traditional song. Updated illustrations help readers see that farmers live in the present, too!

🎺 *Focus on Phonological Awareness (phoneme addition):* As children sing this song, have them add a different sound in front of *e-i-e-i-o* for every verse. For example, one time they can add /z/, changing *e-i-e-i-o* to *ze-zi-ze-zi-zo*.

134

Old MacDonald Had a Farm
Siobhan Dodds, Author and Illustrator
Cambridge, MA: Candlewick. 1999. 0-7636-0761-4.

In this familiar song, the animals on the farm are hidden by a flap. As the song is sung and the flap is turned, children see the different animals that are mentioned. Instead of the full verse, however, only the first part is shown.

Old MacDonald Had a Farm
Carol Jones, Illustrator
Boston: Houghton Mifflin. 1989. 0-395-90125-1.

Here we have the traditional song with a bit of a twist. The illustrations disguise the animal being named, giving readers a chance to guess using the clues shown through a round hole cut in the page. A turn of the page reveals the answer along with the verse.

📖 *Book Extender:* Invite children to create their own pages similar to those shown in the text. Magazines or original drawings can be used. Once they are finished, provide students with time to guess what is being revealed by using the part of the picture shown through the hole.

Raffi's Top Ten Songs to Read
Raffi, Compiler
Illustrated by ten artists
New York: Crown. 1996. 0-517-70907-4.

Represented in this collection are ten children's songs, complete with musical scores and verses. Specific activities appropriate for each song are listed in the back of the book.

Sailor Song
Nancy Jewell, Author
Stefano Vitale, Illustrator
New York: Clarion. 1999. 0-395-82511-3.

In this soothing text, a mother sings a child a story about how a sailor finds his way home from the sea to see his family. Each verse brings the sailor closer to home. After each verse the child responds, "Mama, mama, sing me some more."

📖 *Book Extender:* Although the mother sings the song, the actual music is not included. Encourage children to create their own class melody. Fearful of writing musical scores? Use a tape recorder instead! Have children sing their created melody and record them while they are singing. This tape can then be used when singing the song at another time. Simply put on the tape, have children listen to it, then have them sing along!

Simple Gifts: A Shaker Hymn
Chris Raschka, Illustrator
New York: Holt. 1998. 0-8050-5143-0.

Originally composed by the Shakers around 1848, this song was sung rapidly to go with rapid dancing. The Shakers used it along with other songs on Sundays and evenings as they sang and danced. The lyrics emphasize how wonderful it is to be simple and free. Music is included in the back of the text.

A Summery Saturday Morning
Margaret Mahy, Author
Selina Young, Illustrator
New York: Penguin. 1998. 0-670-87943-6.

Many things can happen on a summery Saturday morning, and that is what this book is all about. Things don't go quite as planned, but the children and animals don't seem to mind. They're having an enjoyable time! Each two-page spread provides verse and pictures telling and showing the happening, which, when combined with the others, makes for a delightful Saturday morning. While no music is included, the verses can be sung to the same tune as "Here We Go Round the Mulberry Bush."

Take Me Out to the Ballgame
Jack Norworth, Lyrics
Alec Gillman, Illustrator
New York: Aladdin. 1999. 0-689-82433-5.

This book is about a lot more than the song it is designed to illustrate. Gillman includes information about where the song originated, the original verses, and historical information about Ebbets Field, home of the Brooklyn Dodgers. The musical score is included in the back of the book.

 Focus on Phonological Awareness (word): Large bold print is used to display each line of the song, which appears at the bottom of the page. As you sing the song with the children, frame each word using your hands to help students better understand that words are units of sounds that can be strung together to communicate ideas.

Teddy Bear, Teddy Bear
Michael Hague, Illustrator
New York: Morrow. 1993. 0-688-12085-7.

Here's another version of the classic action rhyme that invites movement. Take a peek; this is a teddy bear like you've never seen! A note to parents explains how to do the actions associated with each line.

There Was an Old Lady Who Swallowed a Fly
Simms Taback, Illustrator
New York: Viking. 1997. 0-670-86939-2.

This take on the original song is a delight. Each succeeding page provides a glimpse, through the hole that has been cut in the page, of the animal the lady swallows. Of course, the hole gets larger with each succeeding animal the lady swallows.

 Focus on Phonological Awareness (word): The words in the sentences are contained in separate pieces of colored paper, making this a perfect book for helping students to understand the concept of word. Point to each word as you reread and sing the song.

There Was an Old Lady Who Swallowed a Trout!
Teri Sloat, Author
Reynold Ruffins, Illustrator
New York: Holt. 1998. 0-8050-4294-6.

We all know what happened to the old lady who swallowed a fly, but what about the one who swallowed the trout? In this variation on a familiar story, the woman swallows everything in the ocean including the ocean itself, only to release each creature one by one.

📖 *Book Extender:* As this is a cumulative song, this is an excellent book to use for sequencing story events by doing the following: Have students state which animal was swallowed first, second, and so on. A large shape of the woman can be used as can cut-out figures of the various animals. Students could place the pictures of the sea creatures on the shape of the woman as she swallows them.

Children who are familiar with *There Was an Old Lady Who Swallowed a Fly* may notice the similarity in story line. If so, a Venn diagram can be used to point out likenesses and differences while also teaching students one way to compare and contrast.

This Land Is Your Land
Woody Guthrie, Author and Composer
Kathy Jakobsen, Illustrator
New York: Little, Brown. 1998. 0-316-39215-4.

This is the first picture book that captures the words of Woody Guthrie's song, originally written in the 1940s. The pictures take us across the United States and depict not only the various lines in the song but also people and places that were significant to Guthrie throughout his lifetime. The book also features a tribute to Woody Guthrie by Pete Seeger, which includes text and photographs of Guthrie at different times in his life. The music and verses to the song are shown on the last two pages of the book.

What Shall We Do When We All Go Out?
Shari Halpern, Illustrator
New York: North-South. 1995. 1-55858-424-2.

In this traditional song, children perform different activities as they go out to play. The musical score is included in the back of the book, making this a perfect sing-along!

138

What a Wonderful World
George David Weiss and Bob Thiele, Authors
Ashley Bryan, Illustrator
New York: Atheneum. 1995. 0-689-80087-8.

Each line of this song popularized by Louis Armstrong is accompanied by a colorful illustration. Students may not know this song, so sing it for them so they can learn it, too. The message conveyed by the lyrics is worth the effort.

When I First Came to This Land
Harriet Ziefert, Reteller
Simms Taback, Illustrator
New York: Putnam. 1998. 0-399-23044-0.

A traditional song is used to describe the adventures of a pioneer who comes to America, buys a farm, and builds a brand-new life for himself and his family. A map of the United States and territories in 1885 is shown on the front and back covers.

Won't You Come and Play with Me?
Mary Dee Donovan, Adapter
Cynthia Jabar, Illustrator
Boston: Houghton Mifflin. 1998. 0-395-84630.

Based on a street rhyme from long ago, this is the song of a boy with errands to run who gets distracted by all of the playful activities around him. He eventually makes the rounds, which start with the barber's shop and end in his mother's arms. While the author notes that this story is based on a song, music is not included.

📖 *Book Extender:* If you'd like, follow the author's note at the end of the book and invite children to personalize this rhyme by adding their friends' names and their own adventures. Invent music to accompany it.

7

Goofy Texts

Sometimes the way we use spoken language is just plain goofy! Consider some of the books written by Dr. Seuss that use nonsensical words to create stories. Indeed, Dr. Seuss was a master at using assonance (i.e., words in a series that have the same vowel sound) to create stories. Children delight in stories such as these because they *are* so goofy! Children also revel in such stories because they love the language play and the abandonment of all conventions to create new words just for the sheer fun of it. Of course, as children engage with "goofy text," they are learning much about their spoken language as well; they are becoming phonologically aware.

The books in this section play with language in some way. Sometimes the play appears as nonsensical verse; other times it is the way the word or words are stretched across the page. Still other times, the play may take the form of onomatopoeia (words that imitate the sounds they refer to). In any case, all of these books lend themselves to fostering phonological awareness in meaningful and joyful ways.

◆

Altoona Baboona
Janie Bynum, Author and Illustrator
San Diego: Harcourt. 1999. 0-15-201860-3.

Come join Altoona Baboona as she travels the countryside in her balloona! See the sights, enjoy the rhymes, and discover the many creatures Altoona meets on her adventure!

Focus on Phonological Awareness (sound addition): Invite children to speak in "Altoona speak" by having them add /ə/ to the end of their names or other words.

Barnyard Tracks
Dee Dee Duffy, Author
Janet Marshall, Illustrator
Honesdale, PA: Boyds Mills. 1992. 1-878093-66-5.

Using bright colors and simple shapes, this text exposes children to many different animal tracks. Each track is accompanied by an animal sound, both providing clues to the animal that lurks behind the page turn.

Bird Song
Audrey Wood, Author
Robert Florczak, Illustrator
San Diego: Harcourt. 1997. 0-15-200014-3.

Birds are everywhere as this book reminds us. In it, children from different regions see and hear different birds in their area. Children will delight in trying to make the sounds of the birds as spelled out on the different pages.

Bird Talk
Ann Jonas, Author and Illustrator
New York: Greenwillow. 1999. 0-688-14174-9.

How do birds talk? What sounds do they make? This book provides answers to these questions, showing word bubbles next to each of the many different kinds of birds that are shown. Children will enjoy trying to make the sounds of these birds.

Circle Dogs
Kevin Henkes, Author
Dan Yaccarino, Illustrator
New York: Greenwillow. 1998. 0-688-15446-8.

Here are some circle dogs who live in square houses! This book tells of the many activities they do within a day and the sounds associated with those activities such as the lick, lick, licking of a face. From sunup to sundown, the circle dogs are active creatures.

Cock-a-Doodle-Doo
Steve Lavis, Author and Illustrator
New York: Lodestar. 1996. 0-525-67542-6.

Here's a counting book that tells of a noisy farm! All the animals like to make their sounds during the course of the day. The large print on each page will encourage children to join in making the sounds.

Cock-a-Doodle-Moo
Bernard Most, Author and Illustrator
San Diego: Harcourt. 1996. 0-15-201252-4.

We all know that roosters are supposed to sound the alarm to signal the start of another day, but what happens when the rooster can't crow loud enough? In this story, the rooster gets help from the cow, who notices the rooster's problem. Eventually, the rooster teaches the cow how to crow, but the closest they can get is "Cock-a-doodle-moo." It does the trick as the animals wake up. In fact, they wake up laughing! The play on words and sounds will have children doing the same!

Coconut Mon
Linda Milstein, Author
Cheryl Munro Taylor, Illustrator
New York: Tambourine. 1995. 0-688-12862-9.

Come count and play with words at the same time! In this text, set in the Caribbean, a coconut man attempts to sell coconuts to everyone in the village. Children will have fun stretching the words so that they, too, can sound like the Coconut Mon!

Eggday
Joyce Dunbar, Author
Jane Cabrera, Illustrator
New York: Holiday House. 1999. 0-8234-1510-4.

Dora the Duck proclaims that the following day is to be eggday and that there will be a best-egg contest. But what are the mammals supposed to do? Where will they find their eggs? Read the story to discover who wins the contest!

 Focus on Phonological Awareness: Children can simply play with sounds as they listen to this book. Have them try to make the sounds of the various animals at appropriate points in the text. Also have them stretch the sounds as indicated by the way the text is written.

📖 *Book Extender:* Provide a large poster-sized egg shape. Have children look through old science magazines such as *Ranger Rick* and cut out pictures of animals that lay eggs and attach them to the egg.

Four Fur Feet
Margaret Wise Brown, Author
Woodleigh Marx Hubbard, Illustrator
New York: Hyperion. 1994. 0-7868-111-0.

This original text that tells of an animal's journey to many different places has been updated with vibrant illustrations. Come discover where the animal travels without making a sound-o!

 Focus on Phonological Awareness (phoneme addition): An "o" has been added to the ending word of every verse in this story. Have children add /ō/ to the end of every word you name to create new words.

Froggy Plays Soccer
Jonathan London, Author
Frank Remkiewicz, Illustrator
New York: Viking. 1999. 0-670-88257-7.

The latest in the series of six Froggy books, this book follows a similar pattern of having Froggy's parents stretch out his name when they want his attention. In this story, though, Froggy plays on a soccer team and makes a mistake that almost costs him and the team the game.

Focus on Phonological Awareness (phoneme blending): Some of the words in this book are written to convey the necessity of stretching out the sounds. Using these words, stretch out the sounds and ask students to blend the sounds together and to state the word.

Here Comes Henny
Charlotte Pomerantz, Author
Nancy Winslow Parker, Illustrator
New York: Mulberry. 1999. 0-688-16703-9.

Henny Penny takes care of her chicks, even though they are rather picky! This tongue twister is sure to cause a giggle or two as children learn about the trials and tribulations of being Henny Penny. Cluck!

 Focus on Phonological Awareness (phoneme addition): This is an excellent book to illustrate how to add sounds to the ends of words. In keeping with the words in the book, add /ē/ to the end of each child's name and all words when speaking to students and encourage them to do the same.

My Day in the Garden
Miela Ford, Author
Anita Lobel, Illustrator
New York: Greenwillow. 1999. 0-688-15541-3.

What can you do on a rainy day? The young girls in this story decide that they will play dress-up. They dress up like the insects and animals they find in a garden.

📖 *Book Extender:* Provide clothes for children to play dress-up during their free time.

One Sunday Morning
Yumi Heo, Author and Illustrator
New York: Orchard. 1999. 0-531-30156-7.

One Sunday, Minho dreams that he and his father take a walk in the park. They discover many activities going on in the park and most create sounds. The remote-control boats make a "whirrrr" sound, whereas the horse goes *clip, clop*. After all the fun, Minho is awakened only to discover that all of his fun was a "dreeeeeeeeeam."

 Focus on Phonological Awareness: This is a perfect book for encouraging kids to make sounds as portrayed on the various pages. Doing so will help them feel the sounds on their tongues. During a second reading, pause and allow students to make the sounds shown for the various activities.

One Tiger Growls
Ginger Wadsworth, Author
James M. Needham, Illustrator
Watertown, MA: Charlesbridge. 1999. 0-88106-274-X.

Here is a counting book of animal sounds. From the tiger who growls *gr-r-r-r-r* to the twenty frogs that croak *ribbit-ribbit*, all sorts of animal sounds are provided.

📖 *Book Extender:* Encourage children to make the sounds of the animals as you reread the book. Show students how to stretch the sounds when the text indicates that this needs to be done.

Raven and River
Nancy White Carlstrom, Author
Jon Van Zyle, Illustrator
New York: Little, Brown. 1997. 0-316-12894-5.

If you're wondering about the sights and sounds of Alaska, you must take a look at this book! Sounds of different animals that inhabit Alaska are provided as are many different sights.

 Focus on Phonological Awareness: Invite children to make the "sounds of Alaska" as you reread this book.

Run, Jump, Whiz, Splash
Vera Rosenberry, Author and Illustrator
New York: Holiday House. 1999. 0-8234-1378-0.

What do you do in the various seasons? Using simple text, this book presents specific activities that some children like to do for each season. Each season is also described.

 Focus on Phonological Awareness: Many words are stretched in this book as indicated by the way they are written. Provide children with some blending practice by having them follow your lead as you stretch the sounds and put them together to say the word.

📖 *Book Extender:* Provide children with a piece of construction paper. Have them fold it into four parts and draw or find pictures in magazines that show what they like to do in each season.

Small Green Snake
Libba Moore Gray, Author
Holly Meade, Illustrator
New York: Orchard. 1994. 0-531-06844-7.

Sometimes children do not listen to their parents. Such is the case in this book. Snake defies his mother by leaving to investigate the sounds he hears beyond the garden wall. He discovers that listening to his mother might be a good thing to do after all!

Splosh!
Mick Inkpen, Author and Illustrator
San Diego: Harcourt. 1999. 0-15-202299-6.

Kipper and his friends have many experiences in the rain. Many different sounds are created as the rain falls on different objects. Finally, much to their happiness, the sun appears!

 Focus on Phonological Awareness (phoneme isolation): Tell children that you will say two words from the story and that you want them to tell how the sound in the middle of the word is changed from the first to the second word. Sample words from the text are *splash, splosh; slop, slap.*

There's Nothing to D-o-o-o!
Judith Mathews, Author
Kurt Cyrus, Illustrator
San Diego: Browndeer/Harcourt. 1999. 0-15-201647-3.

All children become bored once in awhile and this is certainly true for Laloo, the cow in this story. Seeking adventure, she sets off to discover new kinds of things to do with her life but in the end returns home to more familiar, thus more comfortable, surroundings.

What Baby Wants
Phyllis Root, Author
Jill Barton, Illustrator
Cambridge, MA: Candlewick. 1998. 0-7636-0207-8.

Probably one of the biggest frustrations of being a baby is trying to communicate what is wanted. This is exactly what happens to the baby in this book. From the "pikala, pokala" of the flowers as they prick the baby's nose to the "hushabye, shushabye," many words are created as different family members try to figure out just what the baby wants, and thus stop the crying. Finally, little brother stops the crying by picking up the baby and singing him a lullaby.

What's That Sound, Woolly Bear?
Philemon Sturges, Author
Joan Paley, Illustrator
New York: Little, Brown. 1996. 0-316-82021-0.

As a woolly bear caterpillar looks for a place to spin her bed, other bugs make different sounds. Bugs that *buzzzzzzzzz* and those that *zit-zat* invite children to play with sounds.

Wiggle Waggle
Jonathan London, Author
Michael Rex, Illustrator
San Diego: Silver Whistle/Harcourt. 1999. 0-15-201940-5.

Come discover how different animals walk. Better yet, join in the activity and see if you can walk just like each of the animals shown in this book!

Focus on Phonological Awareness: Encourage children to make the sounds that the animals make as they walk. To call attention to specific changes in words, ask questions such as, "*Wiggle, waggle*. How are they the same? How are they different?"

Wormy Worm
Chris Raschka, Author and Illustrator
New York: Hyperion. 2000. 0-7868-0582-X.

In this playful text, very simple text is used to show how a worm takes delight as it wiggles and woggles. The only problem that this wiggling and woggling creates is trying to figure out which end is truly its end!

Z-Z-Zoink!
Bernard Most, Author and Illustrator
San Diego: Harcourt. 1999. 0-15-292845-6.

A pig snores so loudly that she wakes up all the other farm animals. In turn, each group of animals sends her away so that they can get their rest. Options exhausted, she finally discovers that she can sleep and snore with the owls.

8

Gathering Additional Ideas

Want some additional ideas you can use to nurture phonological awareness at different times during the day? Would you appreciate some quick yet worthwhile activities you can use to fill in a minute here or there while children are waiting for a guest speaker or some other event? If so, the activities listed below may be just for you. Figure 8–1 provides an overview of the ideas listed in this chapter and shows how they are designed to foster one or more areas of phonological awareness. Specific descriptions for each activity follow the chart. Use the ideas as stated or modify them to fit your students' needs. Perhaps they will spark your own creative ideas.

Descriptions of Phonological-Awareness Activities

Count the Words Provide children with counters and containers. Every time a word is said, have them drop a counter into their container.

Cut and Count Write a sentence on a sentence strip. Ask children to watch as the sentence is cut into words and to count every time a word is cut off the sentence. Finally, ask them to tell how many words were used to create the sentence.

Clap the Parts Select one- and two-syllable words. State the words, showing children how to clap each time they hear a part in the word.

Hop and Stop Select one- and two-syllable words, writing each on a card just long enough to hold the word. Say the word to the children, showing them how to hop every time they hear a part of the word. After hopping

Activity	Word	Syllable	Rhyme	Phoneme Matching	Phoneme Blending	Phoneme Segmentation	Phoneme Manipulation
Count the Words	•						
Cut and Count	•						
Clap the Parts		•					
Hop and Stop	•	•					
Sort the Words	•	•					
Sort the Pictures		•	•	•			
Find My Word	•						
I'm Thinking		•	•	•	•		•
Odd One Out, Please!		•	•	•			
Chime Right In	•		•				
Stand Up, Sit Down!		•	•	•			
Put It Together					•		
Hear Ye! Hear Ye!						•	
Sing a Song		•	•	•	•		•
Let's Go Shopping		•	•	•	•	•	•
Lunch Bunch	•	•	•	•	•	•	•
I Spy/Secret Code					•		
Silly Words							•
Mystery Bag		•	•	•	•		
Hink Pinks			•				•
Spoonerisms							•
Yes, No, Maybe So!			•				
Sound Hunt		•	•	•			
Sound Sketch					•		•
Word/Sound Mural		•	•	•			
Push Up						•	
Change the Sound							•
Puppet Chatter	•	•	•	•	•	•	•
Action, Action							•
Twist Your Tongue	•				•		

FIGURE 8–1. *Thirty Activities and the Phonological-Awareness Tasks They Foster.*

the word, have them STOP. Show them the word and point out that words with more parts are longer.

Sort the Words Write words of varying lengths on different cards. Provide a group of three or four children with a set of these cards, asking them to sort the words into three categories: short, medium, long. Once they are finished, say each word, pointing out that the longer words have more parts.

Sort the Pictures Provide children with pictures that have common features that can be classified in one or more ways. Consider these options:

> *Syllable:* Provide pictures that show objects that are one- and two-syllable words. Have them classify the pictures into the two categories.
>
> *Rhyme:* Provide pictures of objects that rhyme and have students group them accordingly.
>
> *Matching:* Provide pictures that show words beginning with a given sound and provide time for children to sort them into two piles: *Yes* for those that have the sound, *No* for those that don't.

Find My Word Write a sentence on a sentence strip and read it to the students. During a second reading of the sentence, cut off each word, placing the words in the pocket holder as they are cut. When they finish, invite different students to come up and select the word that is the shortest or longest word in the sentence.

I'm Thinking Create riddles for children to solve related to a given language feature. Depending on how this activity is conducted, it can focus on several phonological-awareness tasks. Consider these sample riddles:

> *Syllable:* "I'm thinking of an animal name that has two parts. It is furry and hops and has long ears." (*bunny* or *rabbit*)
>
> *Rhyme:* "I'm thinking of a word that rhymes with *bat*. You can wear it." (*hat*)
>
> *Matching:* "I'm thinking of something good to eat. It starts with /k/." (*candy, cake, carrots,* etc.)
>
> *Blending:* "I'm thinking of something that names an animal. It has these sounds: /f/ /i/ /sh/. What's my word?"
>
> *Manipulating:* "I'm thinking of something that tells what I like to do. Take the /m/ off the word *meat* to guess what I like to do." (*eat*)

Odd One Out, Please! Present children with a series of three words, two that have something in common, the third being an "odd one" that has nothing in common with the other two. Depending on the words that are used, this activity can be used to develop several areas of phonological awareness. Consider these samples:

> *Syllable:* "I will say three words. Listen carefully and tell me which one only has one part."
>
> *Rhyme:* "I will tell you three words. Tell me which one does not rhyme with the other two."
>
> *Matching:* "I will tell you three words. Tell me which two have the /m/ sound."

Chime Right In! Once children have heard several nursery rhymes, tell them that you will recite one and they are to listen carefully so that they can "chime right in" with the missing word. Begin reciting, stopping at a logical place. For example,

> "Jack be nimble,
> Jack be quick,
> _____ jump over the _____."

Stand Up, Sit Down! In this activity, children are asked to stand if the words have something in common and to sit if they do not. Depending on the words that are provided, this activity can be used to develop several phonological awareness skills. Here are some examples:

> *Syllable:* Stand if the word I say has more than one part.
>
> *Rhyme:* Stand if the two words I say rhyme.
>
> *Matching:* Stand if the words I say all end with /n/.

Put It Together In this game, you say a word, sound by sound, and ask students to blend the sounds together to form the word. For example, to dismiss students, you say the sounds in their names: "/N/ /a/ /n/ may leave for home now."

Hear Ye! Hear Ye! With this activity, you select a word, say it to students, and ask them to repeat it back to you stating each individual sound. For example: "Hear ye, hear ye, my word is MOM. Tell me all the sounds in mom." (/m/ /o/ /m/)

Sing a Song Use the tune of familiar songs such as "Old MacDonald Had a Farm" and create verses that focus on specific phonological-awareness tasks. See page 126 for a specific example. Depending on the verse, this activity can be used to develop several areas of phonological awareness.

Let's Go Shopping There are many ways to "go shopping." One, of course, is to take a field trip to a grocery store and have children buy ingredients for a cooking experience. Another way to "go shopping" is to have children sit in a circle and tell them that they will take an imaginary trip to the store to buy something. The "something" depends on what you want them to attend to. Consider these examples:

> *Syllable:* "On our shopping trip, we need to find things that have two parts in their names."
> *Rhyme:* "Let's shop for objects that rhyme with *bed*."
> *Matching:* "Let's shop for objects that have the sound /s/."
> *Blending:* "Let's go shopping to find these objects: /f/ an. What is it?" (*fan*)
> *Segmenting:* "Let's go shopping. Tell me the sounds in each of these so we can be sure to look for the right thing: light" (/l/ /ī/ /t/)
> *Manipulating:* "Let's find the object that is scat without the /s/. What is it?" (*cat*)

Of course, the same activity could be modified to "visit" other places such as a zoo or a pet store.

Lunch Bunch Invite children who bring cold lunches to search for objects to focus on one or more aspects related to phonological awareness:

> *Word:* Please name the objects in your lunch.
> *Syllable:* Find something in your lunch that has a two-part word.
> *Rhyme:* See if you have something that rhymes with silk.
> *Matching:* Hold up any items that begin with /s/.
> *Blending:* Hold up your /f/ /r/ /ü/ /t/.
> *Segmenting:* Tell me all of the sounds you hear in *juice*.
> *Manipulating:* Change the *apple* into something you drink that begins with /sn/ (Snapple™)

I Spy/Secret Code Invite children to use a secret code as they speak to others giving a clue about something they spy in the room. The person who guesses correctly becomes the next spy and gives a secret code. Depending on the phonological-awareness task you want children to complete, you may show them how to give the code. For example, to focus on blending say something such as, "I spy something /r/ ed. What's my word?"

Silly Words Provide children with a given sound and have them replace the sound at the beginning or end of their names or any other desired words. For example, to focus on playing with beginning sounds, all children's names might be changed to begin with a given sound. Thus, Mike becomes Bike, Lois becomes Bois, and so on.

Mystery Bag Create your mystery bag by decorating the outside of it with question marks. Then use the bag in a whole host of ways. For example, place objects in the bag that begin the same. After students take them out, have them guess the mystery (all begin with the same sound). On other occasions, place one object in the bag and give students a clue by stating the sounds used to form the word and have students blend the sounds together.

Hink Pinks Two rhyming words used consecutively are called *hink pinks* (e.g., *sad dad*). They can be used to help children learn more about the power of manipulating phonemes to create new words as well as rhyming. Have children create a pair of rhyming words and an accompanying riddle and present it to another student or the entire class. For example, "What do you say to a bad cat?" (*Scat, cat!*)

Spoonerisms Sentences or phrases in which the beginning sounds of two or more words have been exchanged are spoonerisms. They help children see that manipulating phonemes and language is a lot of fun. To begin, use lines from familiar nursery rhymes and listen to children giggle as a result! For example, "Old King Cole was a merry old soul" becomes "Old King Cole was a serry old moul." Once they catch on to the idea, use their own names to play with sounds. Thus, Sam Hanson becomes Ham Sanson. Finally, integrate spoonerisms into the read-aloud experience by switching sounds in some words as you are reading. Challenge children to listen for the sound switcharoo! Finally, invite children to create new names of characters mentioned in the story by manipulating the sounds in the same way that their names were changed.

Yes, No, Maybe So! Tell children to tell you "yes" or "no" to questions. The trick? The answer can only be *yes* if the last word in the question rhymes with an object or person named in the sentence. Begin each question by stating something such as, "Tell me children, tell me, yes, no, or maybe so?" Here are some sample questions to get you started:

"Will a dad ever get mad?" (yes)
"Will Sam eat ham?" (yes)
"Will Kate run?" (no)
"Will the dog get hurt?" (no)

Sound Hunt Tell children that you are going on a hunt looking for specific words in the school or on the playground that have a given sound or words that rhyme. For example, you might want children to find things that rhyme with *look* (*book, cook*). Children could also identify objects that have one or more syllables.

Sound Sketch Tell students that you will say the sounds that can be used to make a word. What they need to do is put the sounds together and then draw a picture to show the word. Here are a couple of examples:

"Please sketch a /m/ /a/ /t/."
"Add /f/ to *ox*. Sketch the word."

Word/Sound Mural Invite students to find pictures that begin or end with a given sound, those that rhyme, or those that have a given number of syllables. They can then contribute their pictures to the class mural.

Push Up Provide children with a set of three or four blocks. Say a word, asking them to listen to it and to push up a block for each sound in the word.

Change the Sound Tell children that in this game, you are going to state a word and what you want them to do is take off the beginning sound and replace it with /m/. For example: "I say *sit*. Take off the /s/, add /m/. What's the word?" Other words that work for this example include *rat*, *send*, and *sad*.

Puppet Chatter Use a puppet of your choice, or if your class has already adopted a puppet, use that one. In any case, have the puppet tell students what to listen for and what to do. Consider these examples:

Word: Listen to my sentence and tell me the number of words you hear.
Syllable: Listen to my word and tell me how many parts you hear.
Rhyme: Listen to these words and jump up once if they rhyme.
Phoneme matching: Tell me a word that begins with /s/.
Phoneme blending: Put the sounds together and tell me what I'm trying to say: /s/ /ā/ /f/. (safe)

155

Phoneme segmentation: Take my word apart, tell me all the sounds: fin. (/f/ /i/ /n/)

Phoneme manipulation (phoneme deletion): Take /r/ away from *red* and tell me the new word. (*Ed*)

Action, Action Tell children to fill in the missing sound(s), say the word, and complete the action. For example, instead of telling them to jump, say "-ump." Model the entire process so that they can better understand what it is you are asking them to do. Have them add /j/ and then jump! Other examples include the following:

1. *-alk* (students add /w/, say "walk," then perform the action.
2. *-un* (students add /r/, say "run," then perform the action.
3. *-op* (students add /h/, say "hop," then perform the action.

Twist Your Tongue Phrases and sentences that use alliteration can be very difficult to say, yet trying to do so is part of the fun. Most children like to see if they can state the twister without getting twisted. And, as mentioned in Chapter 3, phonological awareness is heightened all the while. Here are a few twisters to get you started:

1. Sally sells seashells by the seashore.
2. How much wood would a woodchuck chuck if a woodchuck could chuck wood?
3. Peter Piper picked a peck of pickled peppers.

After they get the hang of it, invite students to create their own!

References

ADAMS, M. J. 1990. *Beginning to Read: Thinking and Learning About Print.* Cambridge, MA: MIT Press.

AYERS, L. 1993. "The Efficacy of Three Training Conditions on Phonological Awareness of Kindergarten Children and the Longitudinal Effect of Each on Later Reading Acquisition." Ph.D. diss., Oakland University, Rochester, MI.

BEAR, D., M. INVERNIZZI, S. TEMPLETON, and F. JOHNSTON. 2000. *Words Their Way: Word Study for Phonics, Vocabulary, and Spelling Instruction.* Upper Saddle River, NJ: Merrill/Prentice Hall.

BLEVINS, W. 1997. *Phonemic Awareness Activities for Early Reading Success.* New York: Scholastic.

BOND, G., and R. DYKSTRA. 1967. "The Cooperative Research Program in First-Grade Reading Instruction." *Reading Research Quarterly* 2: 1–142.

BRADLEY, L., and P. E. BRYANT. 1985. *Rhyme and Reason in Reading and Spelling.* Ann Arbor: University of Michigan Press.

CLARKE, L. K. 1988. "Invented Versus Traditional Spelling in First Graders' Writings: Effects on Learning to Spell and Read." *Research in the Teaching of English* 22: 281–309.

CLAY, M. 1998. *By Different Paths to Common Outcomes.* York, ME: Stenhouse.

COLES, G. 2000. *Misreading Reading: The Bad Science That Hurts Children.* Portsmouth, NH: Heinemann.

CUNNINGHAM, A. 1990. "Explicit Versus Implicit Instruction in Phonemic Awareness." *Journal of Experimental Child Psychology* 50: 429–44.

CUNNINGHAM, P. 2000. *Phonics They Use.* 3d ed. New York: HarperCollins.

DUFFY, G., and J. HOFFMAN. 1999. "In Pursuit of an Illusion: The Flawed Search for a Perfect Method." *Reading Teacher* 53: 10–16.

EHRI, L. 1979. "Linguistic Insight: Threshold of Reading Acquisition." In *Reading Research: Advances in Theory and Practice*, edited by T. Waller and G. E. MacKinnon. New York: Academic Press.

EHRI, L., and I. S. WILCE. 1987. "Does Learning to Spell Help Beginners Learn to Read Words?" *Reading Research Quarterly*, 12: 47–65.

ELDREDGE, J. L. 1995. *Teaching Decoding in Holistic Classrooms*. Upper Saddle River, NJ: Merrill/Prentice Hall.

ERICSON, L., and M. F. JULIEBO. 1998. *The Phonological Awareness Handbook for Kindergarten and Primary Teachers*. Newark, DE: International Reading Association.

FOX, B. 2000. *Word Identification Strategies: Phonics from a New Perspective*. 2d ed. Upper Saddle River, NJ: Merrill/Prentice Hall.

FOX, B., and D. K. ROUTH. 1976. "Phonemic Analysis and Synthesis as Word-Attack Skills." *Journal of Educational Psychology* 68: 70–74.

GLAZER, J., and L. L. LAMME. 1990. "Poem Picture Books and Their Uses in the Classroom." *Reading Teacher* 44: 102–9.

GOLDSTEIN, D. M. 1976. "Cognitive-Linguistic Functioning and Learning to Read in Preschoolers." *Journal of Educational Psychology* 68: 680–88.

GOLINKOFF, R. M. 1978. "Phonemic Awareness Skills and Reading Acheivement." In *The Acquisition of Reading*, edited by F. B. Murray and J. Pikulski. Baltimore: University Park Press.

GRIFFITH, P. L. 1991. "Phonemic Awareness Helps First Graders Invent Spellings and Third Graders Remember Correct Spellings." *Journal of Reading Behavior* 23: 215–33.

GRIFFITH, P. L., and M. W. OLSON. 1992. "Phonemic Awareness Helps Beginning Readers to Break the Code." *Reading Teacher* 45: 516–22.

HOFFMAN, P. A. 1997. "Phonological Intervention with Storybook Reading." *Topics in Language Disorders* 17: 69–88.

JUEL, C. 1988. "Learning to Read and Write: A Longitudinal Study of 54 Children from First Through Fourth Grades." *Journal of Educational Psychology* 80: 437–47.

JUEL, C., P. GRIFFITH, and P. GOUGH. 1986. "Acquisition of Literacy: A Longitudinal Study of Children in First and Second Grade." *Journal of Educational Psychology* 78: 243–55.

Leong, C. K., and C. F. Haines. 1978. "Beginning Readers' Awareness of Words and Sentences." *Journal of Reading Behavior* 10: 393–407.

Liberman, I. Y., S. Shankweiler, F. W. Fischer, and B. Carter. 1974. "Explicit Syllable and Phoneme Segmentation in the Young Child." *Journal of Experiemental Child Psychology* 18: 201–12.

Luckner, J. 1999. Personal correspondence.

Maclean, M., P. Bryant, and L. Bradley. 1987. "Rhymes, Nursery Rhymes, and Reading in Early Childhood." *Merrill-Palmer Quarterly* 33: 255–81.

Morais, J. 1991. "Constraints on the Development of Phonemic Awareness." In *Phonological Processes in Literacy*, edited by S. A. Brady and D. P. Shankweiler. Hillsdale, NJ: Erlbaum.

Morais, J., L. Cary, J. Alegria, and P. Bertelson. 1979. "Does Awareness of Speech as a Sequence of Phonemes Arise Spontaneously?" *Cognition* 7: 323–31.

Murray, B. A., S. A. Stahl, and M. G. Ivey. 1996. "Developing Phonemic Awareness Through Alphabet Books." *Reading & Writing: An Interdisciplinary Journal* 8: 307–22.

Neuman, S. 1999. "Books Make a Difference." *Reading Research Quarterly* 34: 286–310.

Perfetti, C. A., I. Beck, L. Bell, and C. Hughes. 1987. "Phonemic Knowledge and Learning to Read Are Reciprocal: A Longitudinal Study of First Grade Children." *Merrill-Palmer Quarterly* 33: 283–319.

"Phonemic Awareness and the Teaching of Reading: A Position Statement from the Board of Directors of the International Reading Association." 1998. Newark, DE: International Reading Association.

Richgels, D., K. Poremba, and L. McGee. 1996. "Kindergarteners Talk About Print: Phonemic Awareness in Meaningful Contexts." *Reading Teacher* 49: 632–42.

Roberts, B. 1992. "The Evolution of the Young Child's Concept of Word as a Unit of Spoken and Written Language." *Reading Research Quarterly* 27: 124–38.

Rozin, P., and L. Gleitman. 1977. "The Structure and Acquisition of Reading, II: The Reading Process and the Acquisition of the Alphabetic Principle." In *Toward a Psychology of Reading*, edited by A. Reber and D. Scarborough. Hillsdale, NJ: Erlbaum.

Snow, C., M. Burns, and P. Griffin. 1998. *Preventing Reading Difficulties in Young Children*. Washington, DC: National Academy Press.

SNOWBALL, D., and F. BOLTON. 1999. *Spelling K–8: Planning and Teaching.* York, ME: Stenhouse.

TANGEL, D. M., and B. A. BLACHMAN. 1992. "Effect of Phoneme Awareness Instruction on Kindergarten Children's Invented Spelling." *Journal of Reading Behavior* 24: 233–61.

TROIA, G. 1999. "Phonological Awareness Intervention Research: A Critical Review of the Experimental Methodology." *Reading Research Quarterly* 34: 28–52.

TUNMER, W., and A. NESDALE. 1985. "Phonemic Segmentation Skill and Beginning Reading." *Journal of Educational Psychology* 77: 417–27.

WEAVER, C., ED. 1998. *Reconsidering a Balanced Approach to Reading.* Urbana, IL: National Council of Teachers of English.

WHARTON-MCDONALD, R., M. PRESSLEY, and J. HAMPSTON. 1998. "Literacy Instruction in Nine First-Grade Classrooms: Teacher Characteristics and Student Achievement." *Elementary School Journal* 99: 101–28.

WHITEHURST, G. H., F. L. FALCO, C. J. LONIGAN, J. E. FISCHEL, B. D. DE-BARYSHE, M. C. VALDEZ-MENCHACA, and M. CAULFIELD. 1988. "Accelerating Language Development Through Picture Book Reading." *Developmental Psychology* 24: 552–59.

WILDE, S. 1997. *What's a Schwa Sound Anyway?* Portsmouth, NH: Heinemann.

———. 1999. Personal correspondence.

YOPP, H. 1988. "The Validity and Reliability of Phonemic Awareness Tests." *Reading Research Quarterly* 23: 159–77.

———. 1992. "Developing Phonemic Awareness in Young Children." *Reading Teacher* 45: 696–703.

———. 1995. "Read-Aloud Books for Developing Phonemic Awareness: An Annotated Bibiliography." *Reading Teacher* 48: 538–41.

YOPP, H., and R. YOPP. 1997. *Oo-pples and Boo-noo-noos: Songs and Activities for Phonemic Awareness.* San Diego: Harcourt.

Index